PROBLEMS OF AN INDUSTRIAL SOCIETY

## McGRAW-HILL SOCIAL PROBLEMS SERIES

Marvin B. Sussman, Series Editor

The purpose of this series is to provide new and improved materials for teaching the introductory course in social problems. In order to serve the needs of this and related courses, the series brings together a set of stimulating and thought-provoking original volumes which deal with the traditional social problem areas. By covering relevant theory and research, each volume becomes a provocative study of ideas and conceptualizations rather than a descriptive account of a particular social problem. Each provides a theoretical framework relative to the problem under study. Together the volumes offer the instructor an opportunity to develop an integrative conceptual framework for the introductory social problems course.

### NOW AVAILABLE

# PROBLEMS OF
# AN INDUSTRIAL SOCIETY

**WILLIAM A. FAUNCE**

Department of Sociology and
School of Labor and Industrial Relations
Michigan State University

**McGRAW-HILL BOOK COMPANY**

**New York • St. Louis • San Francisco • Toronto • London • Sydney**

**PROBLEMS OF AN INDUSTRIAL SOCIETY**

*Library of Congress Catalog Card Number 68-25652*

3 4 5 6 7 8 9 0 V B V B 7 5 4 3 2 1 0 6 9

C

Professor Faunce introduces a number of sociological concepts and themes and then applies these to specific problems which arise in an industrial society. He provides an explanation for most of these problems and offers a few answers, but more questions are raised than answered. The reader is provoked into thinking about the issues and questions posed by Professor Faunce and into seeking those resolutions which are acceptable to the individual.

The basic theme of this book is that the causes of alienation, ambivalence, and ambiguity in social goals and behavior are inherent in the structure of industrial society. There appear to be a number of conditions which produce an alienated man in society. Extreme specialization of work roles reduces to a bare minimum man's involvement with creative work. As a consequence, man finds the work place a less than pleasant environment; he becomes disaffected in an area of life considered vital to the human being. This estrangement is bound to have some "rubbing off" effects: The individual, Faunce contends, set against his work place may develop a similar posture regarding the community, family, and society.

Another condition which produces ambiguity and confusion about social goals and purposes is the competition for scarce rewards in industrial society. Industrial societies are by their very nature bureaucratically organized and generally provide a system of economic mobility whereby individuals, on the basis of merit, competence, and some forms of nepotism, learn how to obtain prestige, status, and financially rewarding positions. It is obvious that not everyone can make it to the top—a few people become bosses and a great many have to be workers. This division of labor, organized along hierarchical and bureaucratic lines, and with limited rewards for the successful, causes frustration, mental breakdown, alienation, neuroses, and allergies in countless individuals.

One impact of industrial society upon its members is to accelerate change in traditional behavior and values. Consequently, we find ourselves moving far more rapidly than predicted into a postindustrial era in which the major tasks are to develop techniques and skills in handling large-scale bureaucratic systems, to learn to live with rapid social change and its concomitant anomie and ambivalence in behavior, and to reorganize institutional systems and reallocate resources in order to compensate for the dislocation produced by a highly technological and segmented industrial society.

Professor Faunce introduces his book with a presentation of basic concepts such as social role, status, power, social integration, structural differentiation, role definitions, status hierarchy, power hierarchy, consensus, institutionalized conflict, social isolation, and division of labor. These major concepts become the underpinnings upon which the major themes of automation and alienation are described and supported. Before discussing these two important themes, Professor Faunce traces briefly the historical development of industrialization processes and describes how the individual has earned a livelihood from the dawn of the industrial era in England to the modern period in the United States.

In Chapter 2 the author provides a discussion of automation, defining it in terms of technological change. Very few major industries are completely automated. The usual pattern is for certain manufacturing operations to be automated, and if it is economically feasible, automation is then extended to other component units of a manufacturing system with the ultimate objective of total automation. Under this type of system the role of the worker is radically changed. The form of division of labor in preautomated manufacturing systems inevitably creates an alienated work force. Under conditions of total automation, however, the remaining workers will be engaged in either machine maintenance tasks calling for considerable skill or machine monitoring tasks which, although they do not require a high skill level, give the worker responsibility for a larger share of the production process. According to Faunce, most of the technological changes now being described as automation are, in reality, only initial steps in that direction. The overall effect of technology upon workers is apparently quite different in semiautomated factories or offices than it is in highly automated oil refineries or chemical processing plants. The form of division of labor and the type of organizational authority structure appropriate to an automated postindustrial society may reduce the amount of alienation which has been characteristic in industrial societies.

Faunce makes a very telling case for alienation in the work setting and suggests that the inability to develop a self-image on the job is often associated with the inability to develop an identification in the home or community. This is the "rubbing off" effect of alienation.

Students should consider whether alienation in the work setting has a pervasive effect in creating alienation in all other activities of daily living. The interesting thesis advocated by Robert Dubin and discussed in Chapter 3 warrants further study. Dubin proposes that work is no longer the central life interest of modern man but rather a means by which the industrial worker can make a living, perhaps even a surplus, and then develop his gemeinschaft relationships outside of the work setting. While the worker may be alienated on the job for the reasons Faunce so ably presents, he can compensate by developing close-knit relationships with his family and extended kin, union or lodge groups, neighborhood associations, and many other types of social organizations. Undoubtedly the pattern of alienation is pervasive for a minority of individuals. But, given the extensive development of automation and its impact upon an increasingly larger number of workers, there appears to be developing a number of compensatory mechanisms for handling alienation in the work setting so that its negative effects are reduced to a minimum in other areas of life.

Poverty, intergroup and interracial conflict, war, disease, and overpopulation are not necessarily consequences of an automated industrial society; but some of these problems are undoubtedly aggravated by the structure and functions of the modern industrial system. It is difficult to describe with any degree of certainty cause-and-effect relationships on a very broad scale; and although it is impossible to state that automation causes extensive unemployment and concomitant poverty, it is clear that these conditions are associated. Today, in the midst of affluence and a rapidly increasing gross national product, we have widespread poverty and a significant rate of unemployment. To some degree poverty and unemployment are institutionalized and we are rapidly developing a number of institutional systems to take care of an increasingly larger number of families who will be supported over generational time; namely, the underclassed who will never be engaged in productive employment in their lifetimes. This is quite a change, as Faunce indicated, from the common response to poverty of fifty years ago when the individual was urged, often with success, to escape poverty through the mobility system in effect at that time. Although mobility still exists in American society, it does not function equally for all individuals; and an increasing number in the lower strata of society are responding to poverty not with a mobility orientation but with alienation.

In the last chapter of this book, Professor Faunce discusses the nub of the problem for any emerging industrial society—this is the issue of freedom and control. To what extent can a society determine its social goals and develop institutional arrangements which facilitate goal achievement without enslaving its members? To what extent can a modern society drift along and still solve its critical problems without loss of freedom, and to what degree must it make choices by instituting a system of controls?

In any discussion of freedom, one must be concerned with the distinction made by Erich Fromm concerning freedom *to* and freedom *from*. The latter freedom is easily achieved in modern industrial society, the former is more difficult to obtain because, as Faunce indicates, it requires a selection and integration of social and economic resources rather than a simple release from past ties (pp. 143–144). In Faunce's concluding passage, he cautions that "without the development of new, clearly defined goals, social change will be a process of drift rather than design"—drift toward a more leisure-oriented society, leaving unresolved its problems of poverty, slums, health facilities (especially mental health), education, and conservation (pp. 174–175). Goals should be more strongly oriented toward "*human* growth as well as economic growth" (p. 175, italics his). Individual freedom, self-respect, and self-realization are the goals which the emerging post-industrial society may choose and which Faunce finds most desirable (*ibid.*).

In this volume Professor Faunce has made a distinctive contribution to our understanding of industrial society, its process of automation, and the consequences of alienation. He raises important questions about the value changes needed along with development of skills by all members of industrial society in order to reduce the effect of current institutional structures in producing normlessness, ambiguity, and ambivalance.

**Marvin B. Sussman**

A distinction can be made between the problems *of* an industrial society and problems that are found *in* industrial societies. Included in the latter category are crime, poverty, psychological disorder, and, in fact, almost the whole range of human social ills—there are scarcely any social problems from which industrial societies are totally immune. Most textbooks in this area deal with problems that occur in industrial societies but are not unique to industrialism as a way of life. This book is about the problems that are inherent in the social structure, technology, and other characteristics that make a society an industrial society. Extensive division of labor with the resulting segmentation of social experience is one such characteristic. Rapid technological and social change is another. These characteristics of industrial societies make it difficult to achieve an optimum balance between individual freedom and social control and have made alienation a common experience of industrial man. The way in which these problems are linked to the distinctive features of industrial societies is the major concern of this book.

In the pages that follow, we will first trace the social-structural changes that have accompanied the process of industrialization. Particular attention is given to the role of change in production technology, and current technological developments, such as automation, are placed in their historical context. A separate chapter has been devoted to automation because of the amount of concern that has been generated about its current effects and, more importantly, because of its possible implications for the future. Problems related to alienation, freedom, and control in mature industrial societies are then discussed. The concluding section of the book deals with possible attributes of a developing postindustrial era.

What I have attempted to do in this book is to call attention to a particular set of social problems that will persist so long as industrial societies retain their distinctive attributes. A final solution to these problems is not possible through customary preventive or remedial procedures but requires so fundamental a restructuring of the social order that it would no longer be appropriate to describe it as an industrial society. The possibility that we are already headed in this direction is considered in the final chapter of the book. Although only limited consideration is given to crime, alcoholism, divorce, discrimination, or other specific problems dealt with in the series of which this book is a part, the ideas presented may prove useful in understanding the etiology of these problems and devising effective solutions for them in mature industrial societies.

I would like to thank Marvin Sussman for his helpful comments on the first draft of this manuscript. I would also like to thank my wife, Sheila, for her editorial assistance and for the construction of the index.

**William A. Faunce**

# CONTENTS

**PROBLEMS OF AN INDUSTRIAL SOCIETY**

# CHARACTERISTICS OF INDUSTRIAL SOCIETIES

There is a crisis in our age, deeper and more revolutionary than the wars we fight. It is the fact of failure, not merely of government nor of capitalism, nor of leadership, but of an entire culture—industrialism. Our generation is experiencing the tensions of a whole culture system. They are torsions of that pattern of life which has grown up around the technical needs of industrialism. . . . Our problems cumulate in this one issue: how can an industrial civilization persist?[1]

This book is about the kinds of problems that call into question the continued existence of industrial civilization, at least in its present form. It deals only incidentally with specific social problems of the sort that we read about in the newspapers: war, crime, divorce, poverty, overpopulation, unemployment, interracial conflict, or psychological disorder. As pernicious as these problems are in contemporary societies, they are by no means unique to *industrial* societies and are not products of industrialism as a way of life.

NOTE: Footnoted references, numbered consecutively by chapter, appear at the end of the book, pp. 176 ff.

The focus of this book is upon problems associated with those attributes of the industrial society that produce its distinctive character and differentiate it from other types of society. We shall be concerned with changing industrial technology, with complexity of social organization, with rapid social change, and with the ways in which industrial societies cope with problems engendered by these conditions. The social problems with which we shall be concerned center on the effects of industrialism upon the quality of life in industrial society. The major theme of the book is that conditions inherent in the social structure of industrial society result in the alienation of industrial man.

The tone of this book is not as pessimistic as would be suggested by the quotation with which it begins. Although industrialism clearly has had some important failings as a culture system, it has also had some equally important successes. If industrial civilization does not persist, it will be its successes as well as its failures that account for the transformation. The continuing evolution of industrialism is likely to produce a form of society sufficiently different from the one with which we are familiar that it will no longer be appropriate to speak of it as an *industrial* society. These changes will, in part, be a response to the threat of overpopulation, unemployment, and the other specific problems referred to above. Basically, however, they will be a consequence of developments in the distinctive attributes of industrial society, notably its technology and form of division of labor. The problems that accompany these developments as we move toward an emerging postindustrial era form the subject matter of this book.

Almost all who read this book will have had some firsthand experience with industrialism as a way of life and will be familiar with most of the topics to be considered. However, we may speak about these topics in ways that are not familiar. Sociologists are often accused of obfuscation because they discuss familiar things in unfamiliar terms. To the extent that this is true, it is not because we have any special penchant for long words but rather because of the level of abstraction or generality at which the search for laws of social behavior must be conducted. What is familiar to people may be *experienced* by them in an almost endless variety of ways. Sociologists attempt to abstract the common elements from these concrete experiences in order to make statements that transcend the actions of particular individuals and apply to social behavior in general. Therefore, sociological statements about a familiar social situation may be expressed in terms that are different from the way the situation is experienced by any of the participants in it. An example may help to clarify what is meant by generalization in sociology. Several years ago the author conducted a study of social relationships in an automated automobile-engine plant in which one of the findings was that "lack of opportunity for social interaction on automated jobs is one source of worker dissatisfaction with these jobs." Because of the general public interest in the topic of automation, a reporter from one of the news services wrote a story about the study that appeared in many newspapers under the headline "Sociologist Finds Workers Are Lonely." Actually, it is extremely unlikely that many of these workers went home at night complaining to their wives that they had had a hard day at the plant because they were so lonely. It is, of course, even more improbable that they went home saying, "Decreased interaction frequency lowered my job satisfaction today." The point is that this latter statement is a general one encompassing a wide range of possible ways of experiencing this situation. Loneliness is only one of these ways; and in fact, boredom, monotony, resentment, and even anger were more common reactions to social isolation in this factory. (Loneliness may, however, be the most common way in which middle-class journalists experience social isolation.)

## Basic Concepts

The problems of an industrial society will be discussed in general terms in this book. In describing industrial society we shall try to isolate the essential features of societies of this type. The problems selected for analysis are related to these essential features and cross-cut or underly many of the specific social problems with which we are familiar. In order to facilitate analysis at this general level we shall use a number of basic sociological concepts and what may be termed a structural approach, or frame of reference. The reader may be familiar with the distinction between structure and function as it is used in biology, anatomy, or other fields. The structure of the heart, for example, has to do with its component parts and how they fit together, and the function of the heart is what it does. Similarly, the skeletal structure of the body refers to the arrangement and mutual relation of the bones that make up the skeleton. When we speak of social structure, we mean the mutual relation of the constituent parts that make up some social unit such as a friendship group, a family, a factory, a community, or a total society.

The basic part or element of a social unit is the *social role*. The term *social role* is borrowed from drama and refers to the fact that in common or recurring social situations there is something like a script that regulates, to some extent, what people do. The script is usually determined by the traditional ways of doing things, or it may even be written down and formally prescribed and enforced as in the case of the job descriptions in a factory. The way in which we experience this script is as expectations that others have regarding what we should and should not do. In the course of a lifetime we "learn the script" for a very large number of roles and generally act in the expected ways because we discover that it is usually more rewarding to act in accord with others' expectations than to violate them. A social role may be defined, then, as the set of expectations specifying what behavior is appropriate in a given position in a system of social relationships. Familiar examples of social roles are father, mother, son, or daughter in a family. Although no two American fathers may always act in precisely the same way, their behavior is sufficiently similar that they can be distinguished from sons, cousins, uncles, or grandfathers; moreover, middle-class fathers can be distinguished from lower-class fathers because the script is different. Another set of familiar social roles is that found in the work place. There are many ways in which the relationships between a clerk and a customer, a doctor and a patient, a foreman and a machine operator, or a president and a vice-president are the same *irrespective of the particular people who are playing these roles*. Each of these relationships is governed by sets of expectations that exist independently of any specific pair of role players. We may even speak of the social role of the stranger since there are a limited number of things we customarily say and do when meeting someone for the first time.

If social roles are the basic "building blocks" of social structure, the shape of the "edifice" is largely determined by three other attributes of social units. One of these is the form of *division of labor*. We are most accustomed to hearing this term applied to the economic system of a society, but it can be used equally well to describe any type of social unit. The activities to be performed within the unit—whether it is, for example, a family, a trade union, or a total society—can be divided among the roles that make it up in a variety of ways. There may be many specialized roles in which a limited number of activities are expected to be performed in each, as in a modern factory, or there may be a wide variety of activities performed in each of a limited number of roles, as on a traditional family farm. The division of labor may be thought of as a horizontal dimension of social structure or, to continue the construction analogy, as determining the width of the building.

The vertical dimension of social structure, or the height of the social edifice, is largely a matter of the distribution of *status* and *power. Status* is used here to refer to social honor or prestige. The things that people value—whether it is income, good looks, skill, intelligence, personality attributes, or any of a wide variety of other possibilities—are never equally distributed within a population. The result is a status hierarchy in which some persons or positions are accorded more prestige and are deferred to more than others. *Power* refers to the likelihood that others will act in accord with one's expectations and is related to the exclusive control of important functions. The person who is able to make unilateral decisions on important matters affecting other persons is more powerful than the person who must share responsibility for decisions or who can make decisions only on matters of little import. Power, like status, is never precisely equally distributed and therefore also produces a hierarchical ordering of persons and positions. The distribution of status and power may be a constantly shifting one, as in the case of a friendship clique engaging in a variety of activities at which different group members excel, or it may be relatively fixed, as in the case of a large corporation. Hierarchical ordering of persons and positions in terms of status and power is, however, a universal attribute of social units.

The division of labor and the distribution of status and power among social roles represent forms of *structural differentiation*. The *degree* of differentiation of social structure may refer either to the number of roles at a given level of status or power, or to the number of status or power levels that can be distinguished from each other. The *form* of structural differentiation refers to the "shape" of a social unit as it is determined by the combination of vertically and horizontally differentiated social roles. For example, the structure of a social unit may resemble a pyramid if there is a greater division of labor at the lower than at the upper levels of status and power, or it may resemble an inverted pyramid if the reverse is the case.

The frame of reference to be used in this book was identified above as a structural approach. What this means is that we shall be paying particular attention to the degree and form of structural differentiation within industrial societies and to problems associated with change in the form of division of labor and in the distribution of status and power. Differences in these social structural attributes are among the critical features that distinguish one form of society from another. In the next section of this chapter we shall discuss the distinctive structure of industrial society and briefly trace the historical background from which this structure emerged. There is one other concept that should be introduced at this point, however, because it will also serve to focus our attention upon some unique aspects of industrialism as a culture system. This is the concept of *social integration*.

If structural differentiation refers to the division of a social unit into its component parts, social integration refers to the way in which these parts fit together. In other words, it is treated here as an element of the structure of a social unit. To return to the anatomical example used above, differentiation refers to the fact that separate skeletal components such as the hip bone and thigh bone can be identified, and integration refers to the fact that the "hip bone's connected to the thigh bone." In a perfectly integrated social unit all the component parts would be linked together in such a way that none would be isolated from the others and there would be no conflict "built in" to the relations between the component elements. Complex social units such as a large corporation or a total society are never perfectly integrated. In a modern factory, for example, clerical workers and blue-collar workers are isolated from each other in the sense that their roles do not bring them into direct contact, and there are no roles through which they are related in the way that blue-collar workers are linked through the foreman to higher levels of supervision. Similarly, there are conflicts of interest that are built in or institutionalized in organizations of this kind. The fact that wages are a cost to management and income to workers is one example of conflict of this sort. Although there are obviously common as well as conflicting interests between workers and management, the fact remains that a good union leader—meaning one who follows the "script" or meets the expectations defining his role—will automatically come into conflict with representatives of management to the extent that they play their role as it is defined.

The relations between unions and management illustrate the inverse relationship between the level of structural differentiation and the level of social integration: As social units become more differentiated, their level of integration tends to decrease. As the economy has become more complex, the potential for conflicts of interest like those between labor and management has increased. Conflicts of interest of this kind involving competition for scarce resources are common in industrial societies. There is an important difference, however, between conflicting interests and open conflict. Relations between unions and management are mediated by the collective-bargaining process so that open conflict—the strike, for example—is a relatively rare occurrence. The many conflicts of interest between organizations that develop in mature industrial societies are *typically* regulated by an elaborate legislative and judicial system, by a variety of government regulatory agencies, and by such nongovernmental devices as collective bargaining. The presence of these institutionalized accommodative mechanisms represents a higher level of social integration than does the state of open conflict that would exist in their absence. Although these mechanisms may be successful in reducing open conflict, they do not eliminate conflicts of interest: A collective-bargaining agreement does not change the differing objectives of unions and management but rather is a compromise between these objectives. Social units in which there are conflicts of interest are at a lower level of social integration, even in the absence of open conflict, than are social units in which there are no conflicting interests. It is necessary to expend energy and resources in the accommodation of conflicts of interest whenever they exist. It should be added that lack of social integration is not being used here in a pejorative sense, and perfect social integration is not necessarily a goal toward which social units should strive. The consequences of social conflict may be good or bad, depending upon the circumstances and the values in terms of which the consequences are assessed.

It is important to emphasize here that *interpersonal* conflict of the sort that develops when people do not like or understand each other does not necessarily represent lack of social integration. It is only where conflict of interest is institutionalized in the sense of being part of the expectations specifying what behavior is appropriate in a given position in a system of social relationships that the concept of social integration becomes relevant. These two types of conflict, interpersonal and institutionalized, illustrate two different levels of analysis and may help to clarify the structural approach to be used in this book. A concern with interpersonal conflict makes the individual the element or unit of analysis, and concern with institutionalized conflict makes the social role the unit of analysis. In the discussion of structural differentiation above, we said that the basic element or building block of a social unit—whether it is a family or a total society—is the social role. The social role may be treated as the analytical unit even when we are speaking of conflict between organizations. Dealing with conflicts of interest becomes a responsibility attached to particular positions within organizations. For example, public universities compete for legislative appropriations, but this conflict of interest is manifest only in certain university administrative positions and does not affect relations between professors or students of different universities. The important point here, however, is that this is the case irrespective of the particular people who occupy these positions at any particular time. It is, of course, true that universities and all other social units are composed of people. Analogously, it is true that the human body is made up of individual cells. The study of human anatomy, however, need not take account of the cellular composition of the body; similarly, the study of social structure need not take account of the individuals that make up a particular social unit.

Degree of social integration, then, refers to the extent to which *role definitions* either isolate people from each other and bring them into conflict with each other or link them together in conflict-free interaction. People who are isolated from each other tend to develop different attitudes, values, and patterns of behavior. Institutionalized conflict of interest by definition involves lack of consensus. The degree of consensus within a social unit therefore is one index, although not a perfect one, of degree of social integration. It is possible that a *low* level of consensus may occur even in a *highly* integrated social unit if some of the participants within it have not yet learned what is expected of them. A high level of consensus, however, would be evidence that the unit was socially integrated.

We have now introduced most of the major concepts that will be used to analyze the structure of industrial society: division of labor; status hierarchy; power hierarchy; social isolation; institutionalized conflict; consensus; and the two general concepts that subsume all the others, structural differentiation and social integration. The social problems that we shall be concerned with are those directly related to the forms of structural differentiation and social integration characteristic of industrial societies. The term *social problem* is used here to mean any condition that is generally regarded in a society as requiring reform or change. The following is a widely accepted definition of a social problem:

A social problem is a situation believed to be a threat to or an infringement upon an established social value and considered capable of amelioration or elimination by appropriate social action. A social problem has the following elements: (1) a situation capable of measurement; (2) a value believed threatened thereby; and (3) a realization that the situation and the value may (theoretically) be reconciled by group action.[2]

More recent books have emphasized the fact, implicit in the above definition, that for a situation to be a social problem it must be defined as such.[3] The same objective condition, poverty, for example, may be perceived by some as a social problem capable of solution through concerted social action, by others as punishment for sin to be remedied only by divine intervention, and by still others as an integral part of the only way of life with which they are familiar. Even among those who define a condition as a social problem, the definition of the problem—and consequently, the proposed solution— may vary. Alcoholism, for example, may be defined as a moral problem, as a legal problem, or as a disease; each definition has quite different implications for treatment. In the study of social problems it is necessary to be sensitive not only to the various ways in which a problem may be defined but also to the power or influence of persons holding different definitions. For example, change in the official definition of a problem within a Federal agency responsible for dealing with it will have very widespread and important consequences. The change in the meaning of unemployment as a social problem during the past half century is a case in point.

In the sense in which we are using the term, social problems are almost uniquely attributes of industrial societies. Poverty, disease, ignorance—in fact, the whole catalogue of human social ills—exist, of course, in nonindustrial societies. In these societies, however, they are often attributed to fate, luck, or other magical causes or are simply regarded as an irremediable aspect of life. If a problem to be a *social* problem must be regarded as capable of solution through social reform or social change, then it is particularly in *industrial* societies in which this view prevails. Since at least the eighteenth century there has been an abiding optimism regarding the possibility of solution of all sorts of problems through the application of human reason. Jessie Bernard states that the "traditional idea of a social problem emerged first as an attitude of middle-class reformers at the end of the 18th and beginning of the 19th centuries toward the stresses created by the new urban industrial order which developed as a result of the new scientific ideology and a growing humanitarianism."[4]

The transition from magical to rational approaches to the solution of problems will be discussed in more detail in a later section of this chapter.

## The Industrialization Process

**A Nonindustrial Village** In this section we shall trace the development of industrial society as it evolved from earlier societal forms. We shall begin by describing a common type of nonindustrial social system—the peasant village. Although social units of this type antedate industrial society, they still exist today in many underdeveloped areas of the world. Identifying the structural attributes of this social unit will therefore provide not only a description of one element of the background from which industrialism developed but also a basis for comparison of contemporary industrial and nonindustrial social systems.

San Miguel Milpas Altas, a small ladino (non-Indian) community in the central highlands of Guatemala, will serve as an example of both the preindustrial and contemporary peasant village. Although this town is located just off the main highway between Antigua, Guatemala, and Guatemala City, there is no road going to it. Access to the village is by a three-quarter-mile footpath up a steep incline from the highway. The villagers live in cane huts with thatched roofs which line the path as it winds through the village. Each hut is separated from the neighboring one by a fence enclosing a small plot of ground. There are gardens within some of these fences, but the fields on which most of the food for the village is grown are communally owned and located on the slopes at the edge of the village. Subsistence agriculture forms the economic base of the community, which means that most of the food grown by the villagers is consumed by them. The land does not provide all the necessities of life, however, and it is necessary for the San Migueleños to sell some portion of their crops or to work as day laborers on the roads or nearby coffee plantations in order to acquire some cash income. A few of the younger villagers have acquired occupational skills of various sorts and work in the city of Antigua, which is about five miles away. With these few exceptions, however, the people of the village spend most of their time working their separate plots of ground on the communal land, growing mostly corn with a very crude agricultural technology. The hoe and the machete are almost the only tools that are used.

Division of labor within the village is minimal; nearly everyone performs the same occupational role. The division of labor that does occur is primarily within the household and is based upon age and sex differences. There is no resident priest in the village and no permanent political functionary since the job of *alcalde auxiliar* (roughly, mayor of the village) is rotated among all heads of household on a short-term basis. Excluding the few people who work outside the village, there is almost no horizontal differentiation in the social structure of the village except that based upon age and sex.

The vertical dimension of village social structure is likewise relatively undifferentiated. There are status differences within the village, but they are not large and have little effect upon the behavior of the San Migueleños. Whether one has higher or lower status depends primarily upon ascribed characteristics such as sex or age and certain personality traits centering around a kind of reserve and politeness in dealing with others. Power differences are also minimal. There are a few men who allegedly have contacts with important persons outside the village and who are able to exercise somewhat more influence than others. Their power, however, is not related to any role that they perform; in other words, it is a result of personal rather than structural factors. To the extent that there are structurally based power differences, they exist in the slightly greater influence wielded by the older, and consequently more prestigeful, heads of families in the village.

The undifferentiated structure of the village has an important bearing upon its patterns of social integration. Because everyone does approximately the same things and has approximately the same amount of status and power, there are almost none of the reciprocal-role relationships, such as employer-employee, priest-parishioner, buyer-seller, politician-constituent, doctor-patient, or Kiwanis Club

president-Kiwanis Club member, that link people together in communities in the United States. The reciprocal-role relationships that exist are virtually all within the family (husband-wife, father-son, etc.) and do not even extend in any significant way to uncles, cousins, grandfathers, or other relatives outside the nuclear family. This aspect of the social structure of San Miguel Milpas Altas has been described as follows: "There are . . . almost no relationships with any continuity among villagers outside the nuclear family. The social structure of the community, with the exception of some patterned activities related to the church and village government, is best described as atomistic, involving little more than a collection of separate households."[5]

The absence of structural links is accompanied by some social isolation as well. The fences between sitios, or households, serve not only as physical barriers but also as symbols of social distance. There is a considerable measure of reserve in the social relations among most villagers, and there are very few close friendships. Conflict between villagers is a frequent occurrence but usually takes the form of complaints lodged with the *alcalde auxiliar* rather than personal confrontations. The villagers appear to feel that they can afford neither friends nor enemies. It is important to recognize, however, that the conflict which exists in this village is not institutionalized; that is, it is not inherent in the social structure of the community. The conflict is at an inter*personal* level and grows, for the most part, out of petty grievances aggravated by the harsh conditions of life in the village. Although there is, in point of fact, very little competition of the sort that might develop in a more differentiated community for the scarce resources in the village, the level of poverty produces the *feeling* that one must guard what little he has against any possible encroachment from his neighbors.[6]

In spite of interpersonal conflict and the relative social isolation of each household, there is a high level of consensus in the village regarding important values and attitudes, and there is very little behavior that is clearly deviant from the prescribed patterns. The lack of structural differentiation means that the San Migueleños live under very similar conditions and share a common way of life. Interpersonal conflict can occur under a condition of high consensus and need not disrupt it, whereas institutionalized conflict necessarily means dissensus. Also, the isolation of households from each other does not represent lowered social integration so long as they are not differentiated from each other in terms of division of labor, status, or power. San Miguel Milpas Altas may therefore be regarded as socially integrated in spite of the lack of structural linkages outside the household. The pattern of social integration in this village might be more aptly pictured as a set of pegs, each in its place on a pegboard, rather than as a chain composed of many links. The sociologist Emile Durkheim phrased this distinction as a difference between "mechanical solidarity" and "organic solidarity." Mechanical solidarity refers to social integration resulting from the sharing of a *common culture* or way of life, and organic solidarity is integration resulting from *interdependence* in a structurally differentiated social unit.[7]

What are the implications of the social structure of this peasant village for the problems that exist within it? First of all, the major problems that plague the village are not *caused* by its social structure, although their solution is impeded by it. Extreme poverty, disease, a high infant-mortality rate, and illiteracy are characteristic of life in the village. Although the San Migueleños would clearly rather be rich than poor and would prefer health to sickness, there is a kind of hopelessness and a fatalistic attitude toward these conditions. They are facts of life in the village, and there are almost no systematic attempts on the part of the villagers to change them. The traditional ways of doing things are valued in themselves, and the connection between these traditions and the problems of the village are only dimly perceived, if at all, by the San Migueleños. Any concerted effort to introduce change from within the village is unlikely to occur because of its atomistic structure. Where there is no established leadership and no social organization above the level of the household, it is difficult for people to act together to resolve their common problems. Where these problems are perceived not as *social* problems requiring concerted action but as individual misfortunes or as intrinsic aspects of a hard but otherwise valued way of life, change becomes even less likely. Lack of structural differentiation in this village produces a relative homogeneity of experience that reinforces the traditional way of life, while the pattern of social integration militates against any organized effort to ameliorate the problems created by the traditional ways. San Miguel Milpas Altas is virtually isolated from the mainstream of events in the nation and the world, but if any change in its way of life is to occur, it will almost certainly be introduced from the outside.

**The Beginnings of Industrialism**  The peasant village is, of course, not the only form of preindustrial social system nor perhaps even the most common. It does, however, provide a marked contrast to the structural attributes of industrial society, and in many respects it is typical of other social forms that existed before industrialism. In this section we shall describe the early period in the industrialization process in England and analyze the ways in which technological factors are related to the emergence of industrial society.

Industrialism was not superimposed directly upon the feudal social system of the Middle Ages but was preceded by a series of gradual changes which laid the foundation for its development. Probably the most important of these changes was the commercial revolution of the sixteenth and seventeenth centuries, which resulted in active world markets for goods produced by industry in the next century. Techniques of production, however, had changed little, at least by comparison with the technological developments accompanying the Industrial Revolution, between the eighteenth century and the time man first discovered how to use tools. The social organization of production had also changed very little during this whole period. At the time the Industrial Revolution began, the family was still the basic production unit. This was clearly true of agricultural production, in which the vast majority of people were engaged. The manufacturing that occurred was also done predominantly in individual households under the domestic system. Raw materials were either bought by the workers or provided by a middleman, and the products were manufactured in the home and were then sold either directly to customers or to dealers who marketed them.

Beginning in the middle of the eighteenth century in England a series of inventions, primarily in the cotton-textile and iron industries, set in motion a process that rapidly changed the whole character of Western civilization. Industrialization has been described as "the great transformation in the long history of mankind on this planet— more basic, more rapid, and more nearly universal than any earlier transformation."[8] The magnitude and rapidity of the change in the English cotton-textile industry are suggested by the following figures: Output of printed cotton rose from 21 million yards in 1796 to 347 million yards in 1830. Pounds of raw cotton consumed increased from 10.9 million in 1781 to 592 million in 1845. The increasing mechanization of production not only increased output but also decreased costs: the cost of producing a pound of cotton yarn fell 93 percent from 1779 to 1812.[9] As a result of these developments, England reigned as the major manufacturing nation in the world from the latter part of the eighteenth century to the beginning of the twentieth century. That the Industrial Revolution began in England resulted mainly from the existence of a large colonial empire which provided raw-material and product markets; the availability of necessary natural resources in England and a climate suited to the manufacture of textiles; the development of a wealthy merchant class with surplus capital to invest; the presence of a large supply of skilled workers and the relative lack of interference from guilds which resisted the mechanization of production in other European countries; and the fact that the European wars at that time were being fought on the Continent.[10] The Industrial Revolution spread rapidly from England to other countries; and today there is scarcely a nation that is not already industrialized, in the course of industrializing, or aspiring to do so. Industrialism is the most aggressive and pervasive culture system in human history.

The specific inventions that were most instrumental in starting the industrialization process were the flying shuttle (1733), the coking of coal (1735), the use of coke in blast furnaces (1740), the spinning jenny (1767), the water frame (1769), the steam engine (1769), the spinning mule (1779), the "puddling" process of making steel (1784), the power loom (1787), and the cotton gin (1792). There is a historical relationship between these inventions in the sense that each occurred in response to a particular need at a specific point in the process of technological development. The process was set in motion with the invention of more efficient looms. Cotton thread could not be produced fast enough to supply these looms, and new spinning equipment was developed. Further development of spinning and weaving machinery was limited by the use of human power, and the use first of the water wheel and then of the steam engine can be seen as a response to this need. The increasing necessity for metal in the manufacture of production machinery might have slowed the whole process of development had it not been for improvements in the manufacture of iron. Prior to the eighteenth century, smelting and all preparation of iron were done with charcoal, and the virtual deforestation of England was the result. The discovery of the way to make coke from coal and the use of coke in blast-furnace operation provided a major impetus to the growth of the English iron and steel industries. The enormous growth of the textile industry stimulated development in other industries as well. Increased output and the resulting necessity for broader markets provided an added incentive for improvement in transportation and communication. Developments in mining, agricultural technology, and in the processing of raw materials, for example, the invention of the cotton gin, were spurred by the greater need for raw materials growing out of improved production techniques. The technological developments in the textile industry thus ramified throughout the whole economy of England and, eventually, of the world.

Two major aspects of the early stages of industrialization that should be emphasized are the application of science to the practical problems of production technology and the break with traditional patterns of production organization represented by the factory system. There have been inventors, of course, throughout the course of human history. Prior to the seventeenth and eighteenth centuries, however, their inventions were seldom directed toward the practical objective of improving production techniques. Max Weber has characterized the inventions of Leonardo da Vinci as follows: "If one scrutinizes the devices of the greatest inventor of precapitalist times, Leonardo da Vinci—(for experimentation originated in the field of art and not that of science)—one observes that his urge was not that of cheapening production but the rational mastery of technical problems as such."[11] It was not until the Industrial Revolution that the application of scientific method to the development of better production techniques occurred on any large scale. As a result of this process, the rate of invention increased dramatically. In the United States, for example, a total of less than 36,000 patents had been granted by the U.S. Patent Office prior to 1860. During the next forty years, a total of 640,000 was granted.[12] Today there is a very close relationship between science and technology in all modern industrial societies which provides a constant impetus to technological and social change.

The factory system is particularly important in the history of industrial society because it freed the production process from its anchorage in the traditions of a family economy. The result was a rationalization of the division of labor in the sense of a consistent attempt to reduce labor costs through systematic job specialization and personnel selection processes. It also accelerated change in production technology since decision making regarding production techniques was less dispersed and less subject to restriction by traditional work relationships. However, the combination of a systematic attempt by early entrepreneurs to reduce labor costs and the absence of any traditions specifying a fair wage rate, adequate working conditions, or appropriate employer-employee relations produced almost intolerable hardships for workers in the new factories. Extensive documentation of these conditions appears in the reports of English parliamentary committees. Francis Place, writing in the early part of the nineteenth century, states that, "the sufferings of persons employed in the cotton manufacture were beyond credibility: they were drawn into combinations, betrayed, prosecuted, convicted, sentenced, and monstrously severe punishments inflicted on them: they were reduced to and kept in the most wretched state of existence."[13] Most of the jobs in the new factories required little skill, and women and children, who could be paid very low wages, were hired in large numbers. The following description of child labor in the factories was written by Robert Owen in 1815: "In some huge factories from one fourth to one fifth of the children were cripples or otherwise deformed, or permanently injured by excessive toil, sometimes by brutal abuse. The younger children seldom lasted out more than three or four years without some illness, often ending in death."[14] The correction of these abuses through government regulation was an early instance of the increasing involvement of government as a regulatory agent in the economy—a process that will be discussed in more detail in a later section of this chapter.

Another effect of the factory system was to accelerate the population shift from rural to urban areas. During the early period of the Industrial Revolution there was an extremely high growth rate in English manufacturing cities. The population of Liverpool was 4,000 in 1685, 35,000 in 1760, and 552,425 in 1881. Birmingham grew from 4,000 in 1685, to 30,000 in 1760, and to 400,757 in 1881. The rapid growth of manufacturing attracted many people in search of work to these cities. If the prospect of employment was the "carrot" bringing people to the city, the combination of changes in agricultural production and the passage of the English Poor Law was the "stick" driving them from the rural areas. Population growth, improvements in agricultural methods, and the demand for more wool for the growing textile industry required larger arable fields and pasture lands. Under the manorial system, however, peasants worked small plots of ground in the villages which dotted the English countryside. Except for the fact that the land was owned by large landowners or lords of the manor rather than being communally owned, these villages were not unlike the peasant village described earlier in this chapter. In a series of laws known as the Enclosure Acts, Parliament permitted the landowners to fence off larger tracts of land including the plots held by the peasantry, and hundreds of thousands of them were evicted from the land. The English Poor Law, which had been passed earlier because of the large number of destitute peasants wandering about the country, specified that anyone unemployed who did not take a job voluntarily would be put in a workhouse. This set of conditions provided a large labor force for the new factories and contributed to the burgeoning growth of the factory towns.

With the rapid and unplanned growth of the new manufacturing centers and with a population almost completely inexperienced in urban living, the conditions of life in these towns were exceptionally oppressive. Many lurid accounts of these conditions have been written. Polanyi describes life in these new cities as follows:

There was in the new towns no settled urban middle class, no such nucleus of artisans and craftsmen, of respectable petty bourgeois and townspeople as could have served as an assimilating medium for the crude laborer—who attracted by high wages or chased from the land by tricky enclosers—was drudging in the early mills. The industrial town of the Midlands and the North West was a cultural wasteland; its slums merely reflected its lack of tradition and civic self-respect. Dumped into this bleak slough of misery, the immigrant peasant, or even the former yeoman or copyholder was soon transformed into a nondescript animal of the mire. It was not that he was paid too little, or even that he labored too long—though either happened often to excess—but that he was now existing under physical conditions which denied the human shape of life.[15]

Our discussion of the emergence of industrial society has so far focused upon the development of manufacturing industries. The reason for this is that large-scale manufacturing has shaped the character of industrial society to a greater extent than any other single aspect of its economy. Major developments in transportation, communication, agriculture, mining, and many service industries occurred, for the most part, in response to the needs of manufacturing or became possible because of the new production techniques. The development of mass-production industries is one of the important reasons why industrial societies are urban societies. Manufacturing industries were also responsible to a considerable degree for the structural differentiation of industrial society—a point to which we shall return presently.

Industrialization is customarily measured in terms of the proportion of the labor force employed in manufacturing. The general pattern in all industrializing nations appears to be a shift from a labor force engaged primarily in agriculture to one engaged primarily in manufacturing and related industries. However, in mature industrial societies and, especially, in the developing postindustrial era (to be discussed later in this book), service industries employ the largest proportion of the labor force. Table 1 shows this pattern as it has developed in the United States.

TABLE 1. American Labor Force, by Type of Activity, 1860–1950

| | Percent of labor force | | |
| Type of activity | 1860 | 1900 | 1950 |
|---|---|---|---|
| Agriculture, fishing, and forestry | 59 | 38 | 12 |
| Industry, construction, and mining | 20 | 30 | 33 |
| Services (professional, administrative, | | | |
|    transport, and commerce) | 20 | 31 | 53 |
| Other | 1 | 1 | 2 |
|     TOTAL | 100% | 100% | 100% |

SOURCE: Joseph A. Kahl, "Some Social Concomitants of Industrialization and Urbanization," *Human Organization*, vol. 18, p. 58, Summer, 1959. Reprinted by permission of the Society for Applied Anthropology.

One of the best-documented effects of the emergence of manufacturing industries in the early stages of the Industrial Revolution was an increase in the degree of division of labor. This pattern of effects could clearly be seen in England during the period we have been describing and was repeated in Continental European countries and the United States as they became industrialized during the next century. Agricultural societies are relatively undifferentiated, as we saw in the case of the peasant village described earlier. India, with its highly elaborated caste structure, however, is a clear exception to this generalization. Although industrialization is obviously not the *only* process capable of producing an extensive division of labor, it may still be said that all industrial societies are characterized by a high level of occupational specialization, while agricultural societies, with few exceptions, are not.

The Industrial Revolution increased the division of labor in several ways. First, it resulted in the breakdown of craft skills into a series of mechanized operations. The skilled shoemaker, for example, who under the domestic or "putting-out" system was responsible for making a whole shoe, might later be found working as a semiskilled or unskilled operator on a machine performing only a small part of this process. Each special-purpose machine created a new job, and a separate operator was required for each piece of equipment. There are some obvious similarities in the tasks performed by all semi-skilled machine operators; however, differences in the type of product produced and in the kind of machinery used create sets of tasks that are not simply the same jobs with different titles but are genuinely different occupational specialties. Another significant innovation, the development of interchangeable parts, led to an increase in the number of narrowly specialized jobs in assembly operations. Also, the size of the work force required by the rapidly growing factories necessitated, as we have seen, a large-scale shift of people from less specialized agricultural employment to more specialized industrial employment. The growth of cities as a result of the Industrial Revolution also increased the division of labor since a great many more service activities are required in urban than in rural areas. The idea that increasing division of labor through functional specialization improves production efficiency has been a cardinal principle of business organization from the early days of the Industrial Revolution down to the present time.

Industrialization also set in motion a process of increasing differentiation of status and power structures. The initial effect was a bifurcation of industrial society into an increasingly wealthy entrepreneurial elite and an industrial working class or proletariat. This change in itself did not represent increased vertical differentiation since the manorial system in preindustrial European countries had also been essentially a two-class system. It did, however, represent a break with the traditional bases of status and power. The kind of work one did became the primary basis for allocation of status. A man's worth was determined by his work. Max Weber, among others, has extensively documented the ways in which the importance of work in the ethical system of Protestantism laid the foundation for the development of Western capitalism.[16] The job was regarded as a sacred calling, and success at work was evidence that one had been chosen for salvation. Social Darwinism, a secular version of this doctrine which was particularly popular among the upper classes, decreed that in the struggle for economic existence only the fittest survived; it therefore legitimized status and power differences based upon success at work. With an increasingly differentiated occupational structure serving as the basis for status distinctions instead of land holding or aristocratic birth, which had been more important earlier, the foundation was established for the elaborate occupational status structure characteristic of modern industrial societies.

The change in the position of the skilled worker which accompanied the Industrial Revolution was apparently perceived as involving decreased status, dignity, and independence. The loss of status resulting from the breakdown of traditional skills and the changed relationship between worker and employer was clearly apparent to skilled tradesmen, who felt that the "practical mechanic has become a journeyman, subject to be discharged at every pretended 'miff' of his purse proud employer."[17] The transition from selling one's product for a price to selling one's labor for a wage reflected the change in economic relationships and symbolized the skilled worker's loss of status. That the term *wage slave* had more meaning in the middle of the nineteenth century than in the middle of the twentieth century is indicated by the comments of a group of skilled pianoforte makers in New York in 1854 who declared that a daily wage was equivalent to slavery and hoped that "the day is far distant when they [the wage earners] will so far forget what is due to manhood as to glory in a system forced on them by their necessity and in opposition to their feelings of independence and self respect."[18]

For the unskilled farm worker who moved into industrial employment there was not necessarily any loss of social status since he was in a relatively low status position prior to industrialization. The kind of unskilled factory work for which he could qualify, however, did nothing to enhance this status level. More importantly, in the impersonal, urban-industrial status structure, work became a much more important basis for status assignment than was the case in preindustrial villages. To summarize, the major effects of the Industrial Revolution upon status relationships were the destruction of the traditional bases for status placement, a reinforcement of the relationship between work and social status, the creation of many low-status factory jobs, a diminution of the status of the skilled worker, and the initiation of processes leading to the highly differentiated status structure of mature industrial societies.

A similar pattern of effects upon the distribution of power can be observed. The increasingly wealthy merchant-capitalists supplanted the landed aristocracy as primary wielders of social power. During the nineteenth and early twentieth centuries the entrepreneurial elite exercised almost completely unrestrained power in England and the United States. Some abuse of this power along with the growth of a general egalitarian ideology in these countries contributed to the later development of new centers of power to challenge the "captains of industry." The emergence of trade unions and the increasing strength and involvement of government in economic affairs are examples of this process. The principle of countervailing power and the multiple power centers characteristic of what has been called "pluralistic industrialism"[19] reflect the differentiated character of the power structure of industrial societies.

Throughout the early stages of industrialization in both England and the United States trade unions had very limited success in organizing workers. The fact that the workers were mostly recent rural migrants with a very tenuous hold on their jobs, the degree of power exercised by the early merchant-capitalists, and the concern of government with giving the entrepreneur a free hand in order to encourage industrialization all combined to prevent the development of powerful trade unions. The early, often violent struggle of unions to achieve recognition forms a fascinating chapter of economic history.[20]

The fact that unions were weak during this period, however, did not represent *loss* of power by workers since they had little to begin with. The journeyman, the apprentice, the serf, and the yeoman had never been able to form lasting organizations to represent their interests. The craft guilds, which did have some power, were essentially employer rather than employee organizations since they were controlled by master craftsmen who hired journeymen and apprentices and generally marketed as well as produced goods. The guild system had begun to decline several centuries before the Industrial Revolution; by the eighteenth century the guilds were not particularly strong in England and they never existed, at least in their traditional form, in the United States. However, the master craftsman, more than any other segment of the working class, lost power as a result of industrialization. The same changes, described above, that reduced his social status decreased the amount of power he could exercise in the developing industrial societies.

Although the power of the early entrepreneurs went virtually unchallenged, the basic conditions necessary for the later growth of powerful working-class organizations developed with the Industrial Revolution. The existence of common grievances, such as oppressive working conditions, low wages, and unstable employment, while important, would not in itself have produced sustained growth of unionism. The problems shared by journeymen, peasants, or other occupational groups in the past had resulted in only sporadic uprisings. The concentration of people in large factories and industrial towns, however, made possible the communication and mutual reinforcement of common grievances to a much greater degree than in the dispersed preindustrial economy. The breakdown of centuries-old traditions in the relationship of master craftsman and journeyman and lord and serf along with the absence of any traditional regulation of the new employer-employee relations also encouraged the growth of collective bargaining as an institution designed to control these relations. That the emergence of collective bargaining represented the replacement of a traditional framework for social relations by a rational-legal one is an important point that will be discussed in more detail later in this chapter. What is significant in the present context is that, while powerful trade unions did not develop during the early stages of industrialization, the absence of traditionally sanctioned ways of handling the shared grievances of many employees against a common employer laid the groundwork for this development.

The pattern of power through organization in pursuit of special interests is generally much more characteristic of industrial than of nonindustrial societies. Control of economic resources has always been an important power source, and the Industrial Revolution simply shifted this power from the landed aristocracy to the new entrepreneurs. For segments of the society with limited access to this source of power, the development of organized pressure groups representing the special interests of large numbers of people became the common alternative. The increasing division of labor caused by industrialization multiplied the number of conflicting special interests within the economy. Some occupational associations, for example, professional societies, which had been in existence long before the Industrial Revolution, began to take on new functions as instruments of power, while many other occupational associations grew directly out of an increasingly complex occupational structure with its resulting conflicts of interest.

The greater structural differentiation of the emerging industrial society could be expected to have had an important effect upon patterns of social integration. The overall effect was a decrease in the level of integration that had characterized preindustrial society. The conflicts of interest among structurally differentiated social units represented built-in or institutionalized conflict, and in the early stages of industrialization there were neither traditional nor rational-legal means for resolving or accommodating these conflicts. Preindustrial society was everywhere essentially a small-group society. The family, the small workshop, the manor, the peasant village, and the guild were dominant social units and were small enough to permit face-to-face interaction among all the people who were participants in the unit. Industrial society was, from the beginning, a society composed of larger social units in which groups became isolated from each other. The social distance was greater and the amount of contact less between the merchant-capitalist and his workers, for example, than between the lord of the manor and his serfs. In neither of these social relationships was the social distance so great as that which developed later between managers and workers in bureaucratically ordered corporations. However, even the paternalistic company system characteristic of early industrialism represented a step in the direction of greater social isolation between employer and employee. As the differences in the conditions of life of various groups gradually became greater, clearly different subcultures began to emerge within the industrial way of life. The social units which could be differentiated from each other in preindustrial England and the United

States were, like the families in the village of San Miguel Milpas Altas, linked together through participation in a common cultural heritage even when they were socially isolated from each other. The rapid social changes accompanying industrialization destroyed much of this common heritage, and, since the regeneration of cultural patterns occurred in socially isolated units, the differences in the way of life of various segments of the society increased.

At the same time that this was going on, however, the increasing division of labor was making people more dependent upon each other. The peasant family under the manorial system had been largely, although not entirely, a self-sufficient unit. The urban family in the new industrial towns, with one or more members of the family working from dawn until after dark in the textile mills, was forced to purchase food, shelter, and essential services from others. There was also a more extensive interdependence of employer and employee than had been the case in the past when these two positions were less distinct. The master craftsman had been able to produce the goods he sold, and the journeymen he employed were often on the way to becoming masters and employers themselves. Increasing functional specialization necessarily increases interdependence; and the early industrial society can be seen, in Durkheim's terms, as being in the process of transition from mechanical solidarity to organic solidarity as the basis for social integration.

### Contemporary Industrial Society

In some respects, the structural attributes of mature industrial societies represent simply a more extreme form of the characteristics we have seen emerging with the Industrial Revolution. The process of division of labor, for example, which began at that time, has culminated in the incredibly complex occupational structure of contemporary industrial societies. The first edition of the U.S. Department of Labor's *Dictionary of Occupational Titles*, published in 1939, listed 17,452 separate jobs. The *Dictionary* has been in constant process of revision ever since; and although the most recent edition lists 22,028 different jobs, it clearly does not include all the occupational specialties within the American economy. The occupational titles and job descriptions listed indicate the extreme specialization of function in American industry: An "inside-front joiner" is a sewing-machine operator who stitches the first seam that attaches the two front halves of overalls; a "jigger-crown-pouncing machine operator" runs equipment that smooths hat crowns with sandpaper; an "oriental-rug stretcher" uses a stretching device to shape oriental or other expensive rugs; a "gut snatcher, small stock" removes the viscera from calves, lambs, and sheep. Durkheim made a distinction between normal and abnormal forms of the division of labor. In its normal form division of labor produces interdependence and social solidarity; in its abnormal form the result is alienation and anomie.[21] According to Georges Friedmann, most instances of contemporary division of labor would be "abnormal" if we used Durkheim's classification.[22] Extensive job specialization has contributed to production efficiency; but it has also been directly or indirectly responsible for a wide variety of problems including the alienation of industrial workers, widespread status anxiety resulting from ambiguities in the status-assignment process, difficulty in adjusting labor supply to labor demand, problems in accommodating occupationally based conflicts of interest, and decreasing individual autonomy in complex production systems.

Status and power structures in mature industrial societies are also in some ways simply extensions of the process of differentiation that began with industrialization. The pattern of minute status distinctions in large-scale organizations, for example, is symbolized by the type of metal in one's water pitcher, the size of the nameplate on the door, the proximity of one's desk to that of the supervisor, or the kind of clothing that can be worn on the job. The range of socially accepted criteria for status achievement has also been extended as the number of distinct subcultures within industrialism has increased. If it is possible to identify a separate adolescent subculture, a working-class subculture, or a rural subculture, one reason is that these segments of the society have distinctive bases for the allocation of social honor or prestige. The highly elaborated authority structure of large-scale organizations and the proliferation of power centers reflect these same characteristics in the power structure of contemporary industrial societies. The complexity of status and power arrangements often makes it difficult to have one's claims to status honored or to achieve legitimate power—a problem to which we shall return in Chapter 3.

There are some differences between the present distribution of status and power and its earlier forms that could not have been predicted from the patterns that emerged in the early days of the Industrial Revolution. The rise of a middle class composed primarily of small entrepreneurs, middle-level managers, lower-salaried professionals, technicians, and skilled craftsmen has bridged the social distance between the proletariat and the business and professional elite. The middle class is now numerically the largest segment of the American population, and its values are generally regarded as the dominant ones defining the "American way of life." The corporate revolution has also had important implications for status and power arrangements. As a result of the separation of ownership and management in large industries, the control of economic resources and associated power passed from the entrepreneur to the business manager. In the process there was also a considerable change in the ideology of the economic elite or in the ways in which they justified their status and power. The succession in the course of only one or two generations of business leadership from the captains of industry, or less charitably, the "robber barons," to a generally socially responsible set of business administrators represents an abrupt and dramatic change.

The level of social integration in industrial society is higher in its mature than in its earlier stage but is still much lower than in pre-industrial society. Conflicts of interest are commonplace, and we have become so inured to them that we are scarcely aware of how frequently they occur in contemporary American society. Special interests are represented by hundreds of thousands of organizations ranging from the American Medical Association to the Society for the Preservation and Encouragement of Barbershop Quartet Singing in America. Almost every day newspapers contain some report of conflict between organizations representing special interests. And these accounts are by no means limited to conflict between labor and management. They include conflict between a conservation club and the U.S. Department of the Interior over the damming of a river and flooding of wilderness areas, conflict between rival football leagues over their claims to a particular place kicker, conflict between the Southern Christian Leadership Conference and the American Nazi Party over the right of Negroes to live in previously all-white neighborhoods, or conflict between the Knights of Columbus and the Masons over scheduling the use of a park for an annual picnic. Some conflicts of interest grow out of the fact that major segments of American society are socially isolated from each other, live under quite different social conditions, and, consequently, have developed different sets of values and attitudes. Industrial workers and upper-level managers, for example, rarely come in contact with each other on the job; they live in different neighborhoods, they are members of different churches, their children go to different schools, they spend their leisure time in different ways and places, and their special interests are represented by different organizations.

Although conflict of interest, isolation, and dissensus are characteristic of both early and modern industrial societies, the level of social integration of the latter is higher for several reasons. One is the existence of mass communication. The fact that people throughout American society are exposed to the same news-service reports, the same radio and television programs, and the same movies mitigates to some extent the social isolation of one group from another. However, it is easy to exaggerate the impact of the mass media upon the attitudes, values, and behavior of the American public; and the people who control the content of the mass media appear to be particularly prone to do so.

A much more important change in the patterns of social integration of industrial societies has been the development of a "web of rules" that regulates the relationships among organizations and provides institutionalized means for accommodating conflicts of interest. In fact, it is particularly *because* of the emergence of this web of rules that we may speak of the *maturity* of industrial societies. Nonindustrial society was held together by sacred traditions; industrial society is, by comparison, singularly free of traditional controls. Formally instituted rules and regulations are the substitute for tradition in the industrial way of life, and it is only with the advent of an effective web of rules that industrialism has "come of age" as a culture system and has begun to deal effectively with some of the problems that have plagued its infancy and adolescence.

Relations among the social units that comprise industrial society are often contractual relations. They are subject to control by many government regulatory agencies and occur within the framework of an enormously complex body of law; when conflict occurs, it is settled through formal bargaining processes or is adjudicated in the courts. Mass production, mass consumption, and mass communication have created national product markets, raw-material markets, and labor markets and have generally linked together the elements of the modern nation-state—formal organizations, social classes, communities, states, and regions—in a complex net of interdependent relationships. Preindustrial nations and early industrial nations were only political and, to some extent, cultural units and did not constitute structurally articulated social systems. They were made up of largely independent units, and there was little identification of people with the nation and little contact by them with organizations or agencies outside their community. As long as social change occurred slowly, tradition was an adequate guide to interpersonal, interorganizational, and intercommunity relations. In modern nations characterized by rapid social change, extreme structural differentiation, and a high level of internal interdependence, a web of rules, both public (laws, legal precedents, etc.) and private (organizational regulations, specified chains of command, etc.), has become necessary in order for society to function.

The development of the web of rules is one instance of what has been called the rationalization process. The term *rationalization* is used in a variety of ways. In psychology it refers to the process of explaining away a personal failure. As it is used in this book, the concept stems largely from the work of Max Weber.[23] The emergence of rationalism was a central idea in Weber's philosophy of history. He saw the history of Western civilization during the past several centuries as a progression from magical or supernatural toward rational bases of social action and described the process with Friedrich Schiller's phrase, the "disenchantment of the world." It is in this sense that rationalization includes the transition we have just described from traditionally based societies to societies based upon formal rules and regulations. For Weber, however, rationalism involved a much broader spectrum of changes. The "writing-down" process was included in the form, for example, of codification of laws, record keeping, accounting systems, and even the development of musical notation. Rationalism was also used to mean "an increasing theoretical mastery of reality by means of increasingly precise and abstract concepts" and, in this sense, the development of science was an extremely important part of the rationalization process. Almost any kind of systematic arrangement involving a concern with form was seen by Weber as an example of rationality, and he applied the concept in such widely divergent contexts as the development of the well-tempered scale in his sociology of music and the development of bureaucratic authority in his sociology of politics.

There is one meaning of rationalism as used by Weber that crosscuts or underlies most of the others and that is particularly useful for our purposes in this book. In *The Economic Ethic of the World Religions* Weber defines rationalism as "the methodical attainment of a definitely given and practical end by means of an increasingly precise calculation of adequate means."[24] Rationality here refers not to the appropriateness of means to ends but to a *process for selecting means* that are adequate for the achievement of given ends. The key words in this definition are "methodical attainment" and "increasingly precise calculation." There is an important difference between rationality in the sense of the adequacy of means to ends and rationality as meaning the use of systematic processes to arrive at adequate means. The conscious selection of means that are inappropriate for the ends one seeks is *irrationality*. The unreflective and habitual selection of means that may or may not be appropriate to given ends is *traditionalism*. In contrasting the degree of rationality in industrial and nonindustrial societies we are not suggesting that the latter is more irrational than the former. In the context of the specific ends that are sought and in terms of culturally given meanings and definitions of situations, most of the means that are chosen by nonindustrial peoples may be perfectly appropriate. However, because both the ends sought and the conditions affecting the adequacy of means in these societies change very slowly, there is an unreflective, habitual, or tradition-bound quality in the selection of means. The absence of traditional guides to action in rapidly changing industrial societies induces a persistent questioning of the adequacy of means to ends. The view that "there must be a better way" can be seen as a habitual mode of thought among people in industrial society.

From a sociological perspective we are interested in the social structural conditions that initiate and sustain this habit. The methodical and persistent search for more adequate means to given ends is built into a great many social roles in American society. Scientists and many engineers in industry are engaged almost exclusively in this process, and the application of science to industry is referred to as the rationalization of technology. Efficiency experts are employed by many firms to improve production methods. An important function of the business executive is to ensure the "increasingly precise calculation" of adequacy of means within his organization. Time and motion study, suggestion plans, and the hiring of outside consultants are other examples of this process in industry. Rationality is not limited to industrial organizations—it is an essential component of any formal organization. Teacher educators and educational psychologists search for better ways of transmitting knowledge, city mayors spend much of their time seeking better remedies for urban problems, couples consult marriage counselors to find means for improving marital relations, and religious leaders build increasingly bureaucratized church organizations. In short, rationalism can be seen as an element of role definitions in all the institutions within industrial society. Habits of thought engendered by the performance of rationalized organizational roles carry over into other areas of experience, and rationalism has become a pervasive attribute of the industrial way of life.

We have devoted several pages to a discussion of rationalism because it represents an important qualitative difference between nonindustrial and industrial societies and a significant quantitative difference between early and later industrial societies. The rationalization process is also very closely related to the other attributes of industrialism that have been discussed and bears major responsibility for some particular social problems to be considered in later chapters.

Relative absence of tradition and rapid social change have been identified as characteristics of industrial society. Rationalism is a substitute for traditionalism and accelerates the rate of social change in various ways. First of all, the habitual questioning of the adequacy of means to ends could in itself be expected to produce frequent change. The discovery of new ways of doing things is valued and rewarded in industrial society, whereas it is the observance of traditional ways that is rewarded in tribal societies. Rationalism also places a premium upon expertise, and the role of the expert in industrial society generally includes responsibility for initiation of change. The fact that professional and technical occupations have been growing at a faster rate than any other category of the labor force testifies to the continuing rationalization of American society. In addition, the rationalization of technology produces frequent technological changes which, in turn, increase the rate of social change.

Rationalism is also responsible in various ways for increasing the structural differentiation of industrial society. The persistent search for more efficient ways of organizing the production process has, for the past 200 years, resulted in steadily increased division of labor. The rationalization of organizational structure can also be seen in formally instituted and highly differentiated authority systems. The development of government agencies designed to regulate interorganizational relations, the recent rapid increase in the number of independent and specialized research organizations, and the growth in the number of universities and other functionally specialized educational institutions are additional examples of the proliferation of social units resulting from the process of rationalization.

We noted earlier in this chapter that rapid social change and extensive structural differentiation lower the level of social integration of industrial societies. We have described rationalization as the typical response to decreasing social integration in societies where traditional controls are no longer adequate. If rationalization accelerates social change and increases the level of differentiation, the cycle becomes complete. The cyclical nature of the relationship among these processes may account, in part, for the constantly increasing rate at which industrialization has occurred. Once the inertia of traditionalism has been overcome and the process of industrialization is set in motion, it gathers increasing momentum from the mutually reinforcing and reciprocally accelerating relations among the social structural changes that accompany it. The major characteristics of the social structure of industrial society and the pattern of their interrelationship are outlined in Figure 1.

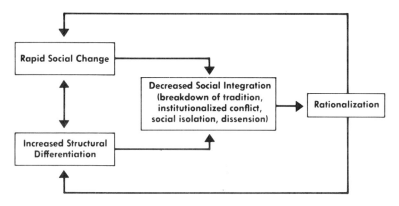

Figure 1. Relationships among the Social Structural Attributes of Industrial Society.

## Social Problems in Industrial Society

Three general types of problems can be distinguished in industrial societies. First, there are the problems associated with the transition from a preindustrial to an industrial social order. Although these problems are most characteristic of the early stages of industrialism, there are some that still persist in the United States and Western Europe. The second type of social problem occurs in both early and mature industrial societies but is not unique to these societies. These are problems such as poverty, disease, and ignorance that have existed throughout recorded history. Many of these problems, as well as those resulting from the transition to industrialism, are being eliminated as industrial societies mature. There are social problems of a third type, however, that can only become worse with continued industrialization because they are inherent in the social structure of industrialism. Problems of transition to a new social order and such ancient and ubiquitous problems as poverty occur *in*, but are not *of*, industrial society. It is the social problems *of* industrial society—those unique to industrialism—that are the principal concern of this book.

Some of the social problems in early industrial societies were detailed in our description of the early factories and new industrial cities. To a considerable extent, the conditions that were described can be accounted for as transitional problems in the emergence of an industrial social order. The time from the appearance of the first true factory, which began production of silk in Derwent, England, in 1719, to the present represents a very brief span of human history. During this period, social change has occurred at an unprecedented rate. Most of the major nations of the world have been transformed from rural, small-group societies to industrial, urban societies. A transformation of this magnitude could not be expected to have occurred without occasioning some important social problems. Among the transitional social problems accompanying industrialization were epidemics caused by inadequate sanitation in new cities, mass cyclical unemployment resulting from insufficient control of the economy, oppressive conditions of work because of a lag between the breakdown of traditional regulations and the emergence of legal regulations, an increasing divorce rate as a result of the changing structure and functions of the family in industrial society, certain types of crime that were directly attributable to the poverty and unsettled conditions in the developing cities, and overpopulation resulting from the fact that the death rate declines earlier and faster than the birth rate in the course of industrialization.

Poverty was mentioned above as an example of a social problem that has been characteristic of all forms of society. It is conceivable that poverty may eventually be eliminated as a result of an increasingly productive industrial economy and improved welfare systems. Both physical and mental disease may also be conquered as a result of the growing amount of energy and resources being devoted to medical research. Mass public education has gone a long way toward eliminating illiteracy and ignorance in older industrial societies. Developments in the behavioral sciences may someday make it possible to curb crime and other forms of deviant behavior.

As long as industrial societies retain their distinctive social structural and cultural features, however, social problems remain that can never be solved. To return to the quotation with which this chapter began, they are the "torsions of that pattern of life which has grown up around the technical needs of industrialism," and it is only through a change in these technical needs with a resulting transition to a new cultural system that these problems can be eliminated. Most of the remainder of this book will deal with three classes of social problems that are inherent in industrialism as a way of life. One of these is the set of problems associated with rapid change in technology. The alliance of production technology with science is unique to industrial societies and ensures a continually accelerating rate of technological and social change. Chapter 2 will be concerned with some of the social problems related to this process, with the emphasis being placed upon one of the most recent technological advances—industrial automation. The focus of Chapter 3 will be upon the alienation of the individual in industrial society. Certain types of alienation will be seen as an inevitable consequence of a high level of structural differentiation and a low level of social integration—a consequence, in other words, of the very social structural attributes that distinguish industrial societies from other societal forms. The final chapter will deal with the dilemma of individual freedom versus social control and the problems associated with the regulation of a segmentalized and rapidly changing society. The issue of how to preserve freedom while retaining sufficient social control to ensure order occurs, of course, in many types of society. However, the form which this dilemma takes in industrial society and the extent to which it permeates the whole social order are unique to industrialism.

**Summary**

The objective of this chapter has been to identify the major social structural features of industrial society and to trace their development from preindustrial social forms. Rapid social change, extensive structural differentiation, a low level of social integration, and increased rationalization are the characteristics of industrialism that have been chosen for emphasis. The social problems with which we are concerned in this book are those that are inherent in the industrial way of life, which means those that are directly related to the social structure of industrial societies. Change in production technology has been identified as one of the important motivating forces throughout the process represented in Figure 1 above, and the *rate* of technological change is an important determinant of the rate of social change. Rapid social change is directly responsible for a variety of social problems in contemporary American society. Chapter 2 will deal with current changes in production technology and with the social problems that accompany them.

# 2

# AUTOMATION AND INDUSTRIAL SOCIETY

A commercial airline recently advertised the fact that one of its new jet airliners was longer from nose to tail than the total distance flown by the Wright brothers at Kitty Hawk, North Carolina, in 1903. In 1954 a chemical company opened a magnesium mill that was capable of producing more magnesium sheet and plate than the total previous national capacity. The American Telephone and Telegraph Company expects that by 1970 its revenue from handling long-distance exchange of information directly between computers will be greater than its revenue from long-distance calls placed by human beings. Dramatic examples of the quickening tempo of technological change in the American economy are not hard to find. Yesterday's science fiction has become today's reality; and as the Swiss journalist Robert Jungk has said, "Tomorrow is already here."

Much has been written about the impact of the automobile, airplane, television, and radio upon American society. While accepting the fact that there have been important effects of these and many other *products* of our economy, this chapter is based upon the conviction that the most fundamental changes are those in the *technology of production*. The automobile, for example, has been influential in shaping our way of life only because mass-production techniques reduced its cost to a level at which it became available to nearly all families. Television, plastics, the electric light bulb, and many other products were invented years before developments in technology reduced production costs sufficiently to permit their widespread use. More importantly, the level of production technology is the major determinant of the form of division of labor; and the form of division of labor determines, at least within broad limits, many of the other important social structural attributes of any society. As we have seen in Chapter 1, the distribution of status, power, and income and the nature of social integration of an industrial society are closely linked to its characteristic form of division of labor. In this chapter we shall extend this analysis to include the effects of some current and projected developments in production technology which can be summarized under the term *automation*.[1]

There is a widespread conviction apparent in the growing body of literature dealing with automation that its consequences for American society may well be comparable to those of the Industrial Revolution of the eighteenth and nineteenth centuries. Considerable difference of opinion has been voiced regarding the specific nature of these consequences, and varying aspects of the first Industrial Revolution have been emphasized as probable characteristics of the "second." On the one hand there is the conviction that automation will mean a further degradation of the industrial machine operator to the role of "button pusher" and that technological unemployment resulting from automation will be "permanent and absolutely unprecedented in the magnitude of its effects." On the other, automation is heralded as the progenitor of the "human use of human beings" and is described as a "magic key" to the door at the "threshold of a golden tomorrow." A pamphlet on automation prepared by the National Association of Manufacturers states: "For the expanding, dynamic economy of America, the sky is indeed the limit. Now more than ever we must have confidence in America's capacity to grow. Guided by electronics, powered by atomic energy, geared to the smooth, effortless workings of automation, the magic carpet of our free economy heads for distant and undreamed of horizons. Just going along for the ride will be the biggest thrill on earth."[2]

A statement by Walter Reuther, president of the United Automobile Workers' Union, at the congressional hearings on automation in 1955 contained the following reaction to the quotation above: "We do not believe that any thinking person is prepared to accept the N.A.M.'s 'magic carpet' theory of economics. Automation holds the promise of a future of new abundance, new leisure and new freedoms, but before that future can be achieved there will be many serious and difficult problems to be solved. We do not believe that the American people or the Congress are prepared to 'just go along for the ride.' "[3]

There are clearly some major differences of opinion about the effects of automation, and the research that has been done can be used to support either side of the controversy. Some studies have shown that automation results in more functionally specialized jobs and greater isolation and alienation of workers, and other studies have shown exactly the opposite pattern of effects. One source of confusion in the debates about the probable effects of automation and also in the social scientific research dealing with these effects is that *distinctly different types of technological change have been called automation.* For many industrial workers, the term has come to mean any new labor-saving device that causes unemployment. In a study done in 1956, over three-fourths of a sample of automobile workers believed that automation would mean a permanent reduction in the number of workers needed and would increase "long-run" unemployment. Twenty-five percent of this same sample of workers felt that the government should actually *control* who uses automated equipment and when it can be introduced in order to prevent any possible unemployment.[4] From the point of view of some spokesmen for industrial management, automation does not represent a significant change in technology—they say there is nothing new about automation except the word itself. In support of their position they refer to a continuous-process flour mill which was in operation in Philadelphia in 1784 and to the invention of a power loom controlled with punched paper cards by a Frenchman named Jacquard in 1801. Social scientists have studied such diverse processes as the use of automatic in-line transfer equipment for handling materials between machine operations and the use of computers for information processing in offices—and they have called both of these things automation.

## The Meaning of Automation

Our first task in this chapter will be to define automation and to relate it to the technological changes accompanying industrialization that were discussed in Chapter 1. Technological development will be described here as a sequence of developmental stages characterized by different types of man-machine relationships. Both office and factory automation will be discussed in the context of these developmental stages.

A common shortcoming in discussions of the social consequences of technological change is the treatment of production technology as a unitary phenomenon. Change in certain production functions may have quite different consequences from change in others. Dividing the production process into its component functions permits analysis of these varying consequences and has the additional advantage of revealing sequences in technological development that would not otherwise be apparent.

The production process can be divided into four basic components with which more or less independent technologies are associated. The first of these is *power technology*, which deals with the sources of energy used in production. A second is *processing technology*, which refers to the tools and techniques used in the actual operations performed upon raw materials. A third is *materials-handling technology*, which deals with the transfer of materials between processing operations. The final component of production technology is *control*, or the regulation of quality and quantity of output. Any production process involving the conversion of raw materials into finished products can be separated into its power, processing, materials-handling, and control components. In contemporary plants manufacturing automobile-engine blocks, for example, the crude blocks are mechanically *transferred* between machines which automatically perform the various broaching, boring, milling, and other *processing* operations. Automatic inspection instruments are used, and, in some instances, feedback devices automatically *control* quality and quantity of output. Since the function of workers in these plants is limited, for the most part, to monitoring or maintaining the machines, the source of *power* for each of the production components is almost exclusively electrical. Examples illustrating the fact that the production process can be divided into these four component functions could also be drawn from situations involving little or no mechanization of production operations.

Technological advance in each component occurs in two phases: First, substitution of inanimate for human performance of the function and second, increases in the efficiency of the machinery that is introduced. Although technological development may occur independently in any one of the production components, *a certain level of development of each is a necessary condition for further development of the others*. In the cotton-textile industry, for example, the spinning jenny had been developed and was in widespread use prior to the introduction of either water or steam power. However, the use of multiple-spindle jennies and spinning frames with a greater production capacity was limited by the inadequacies of human power. Recourse to inanimate energy sources was thus prerequisite to further technical advance of this processing operation.

This example suggests that we may be able to see in the evolution of production technology a sequential relationship between developments in the production components described above. Examination of the history of technological change in various industries indicates that the substitution of inanimate for human power initiates a sequence of similar changes, first in processing, next in materials handling, and eventually in production control. A certain level of development of power technology is prerequisite to the use of higher-speed, special-purpose processing machines. In order to get maximum utilization of these new machines, it eventually becomes necessary to substitute mechanical for human handling of materials between processing operations. The development of conveyor belts and, more recently, of high-speed, in-line transfer equipment is an example of this change. As processing and materials-handling devices become increasingly efficient and as production begins to approximate a continuous flow, exercising human control of quality or quantity of output limits production capacity. Mechanization of control results not only from the fact that the speed of the production process begins to exceed the ability of human operators to regulate quality of output but also from the opportunity for integrating previously separate operations. Automatic transfer of materials between processing stations makes it possible to mechanically regulate larger segments of the production process from centralized control panels, with resulting savings in direct labor costs. We are currently witnessing the emergence of a separate technology of production control. Computers, sensing instruments, and feedback devices are examples of developments in this area. *Automation, as the term is used in this book, refers to the automatic, centralized control of an integrated production system.* The differences between more and less automated production systems will be examined further in a subsequent section where the rate at which various industries are becoming automated will be considered.

### Stages of Technological Development

Mechanization of any one of the four production components may have different social and economic consequences from the others irrespective of the point at which it falls in the overall development of production technology. Our concern here, however, is with the various phases in the developmental sequence that has been described. In most industries, three such phases can be identified. The first is the handicraft stage of production that exists prior to the sequence of technological changes with which we are primarily concerned. The second period is that in which mechanization of energy conversion and processing operations occurs. The final stage is characterized by a highly developed materials-handling technology and by the introduction of automatic production control. It is the linking together of separate operations into a *continuous and automatic system* which particularly distinguishes this third period.[5]

These three phases, which will be referred to as *craft* production, *mechanized* production, and *automated* production, may last varying numbers of years in different industries and may occur at various points in their histories. While mechanization of processing occurred very early, for example, in the production of textiles, there is still little integration of these processes around centralized, automatic controls. Oil refining, certain types of chemical processing, and electrical-power generation are more nearly automated industries where, in some instances, basic changes in processing, materials handling, and control took place almost simultaneously. Mechanization of processing and materials handling in the automobile, steel, and rubber industries has just recently reached a point where it is becoming not only feasible but also increasingly necessary to introduce automatic controls.

The three stages of technological development are most apparent when we examine broad trends in the history of production technology. In the short run and in particular industries this pattern of change may not always occur. One way in which the pattern may be obscured is through the introduction of machines or other hardware characteristic of a particular stage prior to the other developments that make their use necessary or appropriate. Computers are being introduced today for a wide variety of reasons, including in some cases the desire to appear up to date. It is not the specific hardware in use, but the way in which it is used that distinguishes one stage of technological development from another. Only the use of computers as integrating control devices fits our definition of automation.

In spite of these variations, stages of development can be identified in almost all industries, and there appears to be a unique man-machine relationship that is characteristic of each period. In the handicraft stage of production, tools are an adjunct to the skill of the craftsman, and it is primarily his ability and not his equipment that determines the quality and quantity of his output. With the mechanization of processing operations, however, skill is increasingly built into the machines. Mumford has described the difference between machines and tools as lying in the "degree of independence in the operation from the skill and motive power of the operator: the tool lends itself to manipulation, the machine to automatic action."[6] As was noted in Chapter 1, the Industrial Revolution of the eighteenth century had the frequently noted and well-documented effect of replacing skilled, tool-using artisans with semiskilled machine operators.

With the advent of automation there appears to be another basic change in the man-machine relationship. We have briefly described the transition from the craftsman as a skilled manipulator of tools to the industrial worker as an operator of a special-purpose machine. In the automated plant the worker is increasingly a *monitor* of a *group* of special-purpose machines and, in some instances, of a completely integrated production system. His responsibility may be limited to watching a panel of lights or gauges that indicate whether all production components are functioning as expected. He does not initiate processing operations, nor does he have any control of quality or quantity of output. Materials handling between processing stations is automatic, and the substitution of inanimate for human energy used directly in production is virtually complete.

We have so far been concerned primarily with technological change in manufacturing operations. Studies of the introduction of electronic data-processing systems in offices suggest a somewhat different pattern of effects than that associated with factory automation. Analyzing work performed in offices in terms of its component functions and in terms of various developmental phases in the relationship between office workers and office machines may help in understanding this difference.

There is at least an analogy between the four production components discussed above and the elements of office work. The flow of work in the office is primarily a flow of information that must be transferred in some way between processing operations. Included in these processing operations is a wide variety of activities, such as information storage or filing, changing the form of information as in typing or keypunching, adding to the amount of information, and sorting it in ways that make it more meaningful. The major end products of this work are decisions of various sorts. Control within the total system is a matter of regulation of the "quality" of decisions in the sense of their correctness and of the "quantity" of decisions in the sense of the speed with which they can be made. Some source of energy is, of course, required for any activity.

As in the factory, each of the component functions of office work may be performed by human beings or by machines, and the level of mechanization of each function may vary. There also appear to be similar phases in the relationship between men and machines, and these phases are apparently associated with mechanization of the same components.

Until fairly recently the stage of development of most office work was comparable to that described above as the handicraft period. The equipment in use did not have skills built into it but was an adjunct to whatever ability was required of the office worker. The typewriter is an example of equipment of this kind. In recent years the increasing use of more complex business machines has made semiskilled machine operators of many office workers. The substitution of keypunch operators and tabulating-machine operators for clerks and bookkeepers is certainly reminiscent of the changes accompanying the mechanization of manufacturing. The initial impact of such office machinery as card sorters, key punchers, and tabulators upon man-machine relationships appears to be similar to that associated with factory mechanization involving the breakdown of previous skills into job classifications tied to particular, special-purpose machines.

Current developments such as the use of computers appear to be *increasing* the number of people in job classifications of this type because they increase the need for operators of equipment peripheral to the computer, such as converters, printers, and key punchers. The similarity in the functions performed by lower-level clerical workers to those performed by industrial workers in the period of mechanized production is suggested by the following quotation: "After the conversion (to a computer), the detailed repetitive work of this function was done by machines, and the job of the clerks was either to *control* the accuracy of the work performed by the machines, or to *operate* the machines themselves."[7]

The discussion thus far suggests that what has been called office "automation" might more appropriately be seen as a major advance in the *mechanization* of information processing. Most computers in use today perform primarily a processing function and are not part of a technologically integrated system. Computer technology, however, makes *possible* a system in which all information necessary for the management of an organization is stored and automatically retrieved and processed when required. Improvements in data input and output procedures will undoubtedly eliminate the peripheral processing operations. The printing out of information coming from the computer is increasingly tied directly into the computer system so that an operator of separate printing equipment is no longer necessary. This example of elimination of a functionally specialized task through the integration of production processes is a direct equivalent of factory automation as described above. The specific relationships suggested in the preceding pages are summarized in Table 2.

TABLE 2.  Relationship of Production Technology to Man-machine Relationships

| Stage of mechanization of production components | Phase in man-machine relationship |
|---|---|
| 1. *Power source*: animate<br>2. *Processing procedures*: tools and simple machines<br>3. *Materials-handling procedures*: not mechanized<br>4. *Control procedures*: not mechanized | *Craft production* (worker as skilled artisan) |
| 1. *Power source*: inanimate<br>2. *Processing procedures*: low-speed, special-purpose machines<br>3. *Materials-handling procedures*: early stages of mechanization<br>4. *Control*: not mechanized | *Mechanized production* (worker as machine operator) |
| 1. *Power source*: inanimate<br>2. *Processing procedures*: high-speed, multi-purpose machines<br>3. *Materials-handling procedures*: automatic<br>4. *Control*: automatic | *Automated production* (worker as machine monitor) |

Automation, then, in both factory and office means the *automatic control* of an *integrated production system*. As it is used here, the term does not refer to specific pieces of equipment such as computers or feedback devices but to a particular *function*—production control—that they can perform if the mechanization of power, processing, and materials handling has reached a stage which permits the integration of production processes. In this sense, there are relatively few industries that have achieved a high level of automation, although many industries can be seen as moving in this direction.

An oil refinery is one of the best examples of an automatic centrally controlled production system. Crude oil is brought into the refinery by pipeline, tank car, or barge; controls are preset to produce the desired end product; the crude oil flows continuously through a series of processing operations; and one or more products are discharged back into pipelines, tank cars, or barges. The only human involvement in the process is the presetting of the controls, monitoring of control panels that indicate whether the operations are being performed correctly, and maintenance and repair of equipment. The control systems that operate during a space flight are an example of information processing that approximates automation as defined above. From the beginning of a countdown until the return of the spaceship to earth, an enormous volume of information is fed automatically and continuously into computers which process the information and, in effect, make decisions about the flight. In some instances, the process is completely automatic in the sense that adjustments in equipment are made on command directly from the computer. Even where the information goes from the computer to a flight-control officer, many decisions are still somewhat automatic in that there are predetermined response patterns depending upon the information received.

When the "raw material" involved is either a liquid or information, as in the two examples above, the development of integrated, continuous-flow processing and materials-handling operations is somewhat easier to achieve than in fabricating industries involving metal or other solid materials. Nevertheless there are examples of factories in these industries that come close to the degree of automation found in oil refining. U.S. Industries, Incorporated, operates a highly auto-mated plant producing 155-mm cannon shells. At this plant, lengths of square metal stock are unloaded from freight cars by lift trucks and placed directly on automatic conveyors that take the stock to saws where the bars are cut to the appropriate size. From the time the bars leave the freight cars until they emerge at the other end of the plant as finished shells they are not handled by workers. There are actually no machine operators in this plant in the traditional sense of that designation. The workers are essentially machine attendants who monitor control panels. The following is a description of this factory in operation:

It is impressive to watch this tremendous plant operating and to listen to the sounds of the metal being worked in so many ways at such a rapid pace, to see the whole operation being conducted through stations through-out the plant, full of blinking lights and clicking relays, attended by one or two men at each station. The control stations are actually a type of computer mechanism and are interconnected so that trouble in any depart-ment is relayed forward and back along the line and the equipment is automatically slowed down or completely stopped, as each case requires, until the trouble spot has been corrected (in a good example of what is commonly called "feed-back"). This work too is done by computer con-trolling mechanisms and is indicated by them to the control operators by means of varying combinations of lines of colored light. . . .[8]

We have devoted considerable space to defining automation, giving illustrations of automated processes, and describing the place of auto-mation in the history of production technology. The emphasis in these pages has been upon the integration of total production systems around automatic controls. The reason for emphasizing this concep-tion of automation is that its effects and the kinds of problems it occasions appear to be both quantitatively and qualitatively different from the effects of other developments that have also been called automation. For example, studies of the use of computers to perform limited functions in offices and of so-called "Detroit automation," or the use of in-line transfer machines in connection with feedback devices, show a different pattern of effects from those found in oil refineries, chemical-processing plants, or more highly integrated information-processing systems in offices. The difference between the problems created by mechanization and those created by automation is the subject of most of the rest of this chapter. First, however, because the rapidity of technological change determines the magnitude of many of the social problems it produces, we shall attempt to assess the rate at which we are entering the "age of automation."

## Rate of Development of Automation

In the sense that we are using the term, the automation of American industry has just begun, and only a small proportion of factories and offices could be described as automated. The rate at which automation develops and is diffused into new industries in the future will have an important bearing upon the nature and extent of the problems it produces. In Table 3 most major American industries have been classified in terms of their position in the sequence of technological developments leading to automation. Because there is no precise way of ranking industries along this continuum, the classification in Table 3 is necessarily somewhat arbitrary. It is based primarily upon the extent to which factory or office operations are integrated around centralized, automatic controls and also upon the specific types of technological innovations that are presently occurring in the industry. The level of automation of the most advanced factories or offices in an industry served as the basis for assigning it to a category, although some weight was also given to the proportion of factories or offices in the industry that are at various stages of automation. Although there are varying levels of technological development among the plants in some industries, the assumption has been made in this classification that the competitive advantage of moving closer to automation would eventually force the less-automated plants to follow.

The industries in category I are generally characterized by a high level of integration in the sense that the total production process can be regulated from a centralized control station. The innovations that are occurring are primarily improvements in control mechanisms involving the use of computers. The category II industries are ones

**TABLE 3. Level of Automation of Major American Industries**

| I Advanced automation | | II Beginning automation | | III Advanced mechanization | | IV Beginning mechanization | |
|---|---|---|---|---|---|---|---|
| Industry | % of total employment, 1964 | Industry | % of total employment, 1964 | Industry | % of total employment, 1964 | Industry | % of total employment, 1964 |
| Petroleum refining | 0.3 | Cigarettes | 0.05 | Agriculture | 6.8 | Apparel | 1.9 |
| Electric power | 0.4 | Ordnance and accessories | 0.4 | Textiles | 1.3 | Contract construction | 4.3 |
| Industrial chemicals, plastics, and synthetics | 0.7 | Paper and pulp | 0.3 | Food processing (except milk and beverages) | 1.9 | Wholesale and retail trade | 17.2 |
| Cement, hydraulic | 0.05 | Chemicals (except industrial, plastics, or synthetics) | 0.6 | Rubber | 0.6 | Transportation | 3.5 |
| | | Glass containers | 0.08 | Motor vehicle | 1.1 | Finance and real estate (except banking) | 1.9 |
| | | Milk | 0.3 | Aircraft and missile | 0.9 | Services | 12.2 |
| | | Beverages | 0.3 | Primary metals | 1.7 | | |
| | | Telephone communication | 1.0 | Mining | 0.9 | | |
| | | Banking | 1.1 | Furniture | 0.6 | | |
| | | Concrete, gypsum, and plastic products | 0.2 | Printing | 1.4 | | |
| | | Gas utilities | 0.2 | Leather and leather products | 0.5 | | |
| | | | | Fabricated metal products | 1.7 | | |
| | | | | Machinery | 2.3 | | |
| | | | | Instruments | 0.5 | | |
| | | | | Insurance | 1.3 | | |
| | | | | Lumber and wood products | 0.9 | | |
| | | | | Electrical equipment | 2.2 | | |
| | | | | Tobacco manufacturers (except cigarettes) | 0.07 | | |

in which major segments of factory or office operations have been automated, but they are less completely integrated than those in category I. There is also a somewhat greater difference between the most and the least technologically advanced firms than in category I. The major technological developments occurring in these industries are the increasing use of computers and improvements in measuring and other sensing instruments. Some further refinement of processing and materials-handling processes along with changes in product design which facilitate continuous processing are also taking place. Category III is the most heterogeneous of the four categories. The most important attribute shared by these industries is that relatively small segments of the total production process are automatically controlled, although there is a generally high level of mechanization of individual processing and materials-handling procedures. Some of these industries, however, are beginning to approximate a continuous flow of operations involving a larger proportion of the total production process, as, for example, in the case of textiles, some types of food processing, rubber, iron, and steel. Other category III industries, notably agriculture, are unlikely to develop in the direction of automation in the foreseeable future. The major technological innovations in these industries are an increasing use of automatic measuring and other sensing instruments and improvements in processing and materials-handling techniques. The industries in category IV are in the stage of the developmental sequence at which changes occur primarily in the processing component of production. There is very little mechanization of any kind in some of these industries, and the possibility that any of them will move rapidly toward automation appears remote.

The industries classified in Table 3 include approximately three-fourths of the employed civilian labor force. The major occupational categories excluded are Federal, state, and local government employees, who constitute 13.6 percent of employed civilian workers, and the self-employed, who represent another 8.9 percent. It is clear from Table 3 that only a small proportion of the labor force is employed in industries at either the beginning or the advanced stages of automation; 1.45 percent of total employment is in category I industries and 4.53 percent in category II. Even if we consider the employees in those industries from category III which appear to be moving most rapidly toward automation—printing, rubber, insurance, machinery, textiles, primary metals, motor vehicles, aircraft and missiles, and food-processing industries such as grain mills and bakeries—an additional 11.2 percent is all that would be added to the proportion of the civilian labor force most directly affected by automation. Forty-one percent of employed persons are in category IV industries. Taking account of self-employed persons and large numbers of government employees such as teachers who might also appropriately be classified in category IV, it is apparent that well over half of the employed civilian labor force is in industries that are developing very slowly, if at all, toward automation.

The predictions made in the early 1950s that there would be rapid and drastic changes in our economy and society as a result of automation—an M.I.T. professor predicted that factories would be fully automated in ten years—do not appear to be warranted. One argument advanced at that time was that a dramatic acceleration of the rate of change in production technology was occurring, that, as a consequence, rapid shifts in the distribution of the labor force among occupations and industries would take place, and that the institutional structure of the society, which was changing more slowly, would be inadequate to cope with these changes. The best index of rate of change in production technology, although it is far from perfect, is change in productivity or in output per man-hour (the volume of final output of goods and services produced in a year divided by the number of man-hours worked in the year). The average rate of growth of productivity for the thirty-five years preceding the end of World War II, which includes the Depression decade of the 1930s, was 2 percent. For the period between 1947 and 1965, the average rate of productivity growth per year has been 3.2 percent. Although these figures do suggest an accelerating rate of technological change, they do not represent change of the magnitude predicted earlier by either the prophets of doom or the prophets of an automated utopia.

Further evidence regarding the pace at which technological change is occurring can be seen in the changing occupational distribution of the labor force. Tables 2 and 3 indicate the direction and rate of change in our occupational structure since 1947—the period during which most automation has occurred. The long-term shift away from blue-collar and toward white-collar jobs is clearly continuing. The growth in the professional and technical category has been particularly great; and although the proportion of all blue-collar jobs has declined, the major decline, as in the past, has been among farm workers. These changes do not, however, appear to be occurring at an increasing rate. The index of net redistribution of the labor force in Table 3 is a measure of the extent of dissimilarity in the occupational structure between any two years. For the 1947–1948 period, for example, 0.13 percent of the labor force would have to change jobs in order to make the proportion of the labor force in each occupational category in one year identical to that in the other. The higher the index of net redistribution is for any two-year period, the greater is the amount of change in the occupational structure that occurred during that period. If the increasing rate of technological development was producing an accelerated rate of change in the occupational composition of the labor force, the index of net redistribution should have become increasingly higher from the 1947–1948 period to the 1964–1965 period. In fact, the reverse appears to be the case. There has been relatively greater stability in our occupational structure since 1958 than in the preceding years.[9] One reason for this may be the fact that there has been a leveling off of the introduction of automation in the consumer–durable goods industries since the peak period between 1950 and 1958.[10] Most of these industries are at the stage of advanced mechanization (category III in Table 3); and during this earlier period, many were making rapid strides toward achieving more integrated production processes. Further developments in processing and materials-handling techniques will need to occur before more highly integrated and automatically controlled production systems will be feasible in these industries. In the automobile industry, for example, the difficulty in maintaining and repairing in-line transfer equipment—with electrical circuits and hydraulic lines spread out over a machine that may be

**TABLE 4. Percent Distribution of Employed Persons, by Occupational Groups, 1947–1975**

| Occupational group | 1947 | 1951 | 1956 | 1961 | 1965 | 1975* |
|---|---|---|---|---|---|---|
| White-collar workers | 34.9 | 36.8 | 39.4 | 43.6 | 44.5 | 48.3 |
| Professional, technical, and kindred | 6.6 | 7.9 | 9.4 | 11.5 | 12.3 | 14.9 |
| Managers, officials, and proprietors (except farm) | 10.0 | 10.2 | 10.1 | 10.7 | 10.2 | 10.4 |
| Clerical and kindred | 12.4 | 12.6 | 13.6 | 14.8 | 15.5 | 16.5 |
| Sales workers | 5.9 | 6.2 | 6.3 | 6.6 | 6.5 | 6.5 |
| Blue-collar workers | 40.7 | 41.1 | 38.8 | 35.7 | 36.7 | 33.7 |
| Craftsmen, foremen, and kindred | 13.4 | 13.9 | 13.4 | 12.9 | 12.8 | 12.8 |
| Operatives and kindred | 21.2 | 20.7 | 19.7 | 17.6 | 18.6 | 16.7 |
| Laborers (except farm and mine) | 6.1 | 6.5 | 5.7 | 5.2 | 5.3 | 4.2 |
| Service workers | 10.4 | 10.8 | 11.7 | 12.9 | 12.9 | 14.1 |
| Private household workers | 3.0 | 3.1 | 3.3 | 3.5 | 3.1 | — |
| Service workers (except private household) | 7.4 | 7.7 | 8.4 | 9.5 | 9.8 | — |
| Farm workers | 14.0 | 11.3 | 10.1 | 7.8 | 5.9 | 3.9 |
| Farmers and farm managers | 8.6 | 6.6 | 5.6 | 4.1 | 3.1 | — |
| Farm laborers and foremen | 5.4 | 4.7 | 4.5 | 3.7 | 2.8 | — |

* 1975 projections made by the U.S. Department of Labor, Cf. U.S. Department of Labor, Bureau of Labor Statistics, *America's Industrial and Occupational Manpower Requirements, 1964–1975*

SOURCE: *Manpower Report of the President*, March 1966.

TABLE 5.  Net Distribution of Occupational Structure, 1947–1965

| Year | 1947 –48 | 1948 –49 | 1949 –50 | 1950 –51 | 1951 –52 | 1952 –53 | 1953 –54 | 1954 –55 | 1955 –56 | 1956 –57 | 1957 –58 | 1958 –59 | 1959 –60 | 1960 –61 | 1961 –62 | 1962 –63 | 1963 –64 | 1964 –65 |
|---|---|---|---|---|---|---|---|---|---|---|---|---|---|---|---|---|---|---|
| Index of net redistribution* | .13 | .15 | .11 | .22 | .14 | .17 | .13 | .09 | .10 | .13 | .20 | .05 | .11 | .08 | .08 | .07 | .07 | .09 |

* Computed as the index of dissimilarity between the occupational distributions for any two years. The index is one-half the sum of the absolute values of the differences between the occupational differences for any two years, taken occupation by occupation. The occupational categories that were compared were those in Table 4. Cf. Albert J. Reiss, Jr., "Change in the Occupational Structure of the United States, 1910 to 1950," in Paul K. Hatt and Albert J. Reiss, Jr., *Cities and Society*, The Free Press of Glencoe, New York, 1959, p. 425.

a city block long—has been a stumbling block to additional integration of machining operations. Also, the kind of machinery required to perform the enormous variety of assembly operations in an automobile plant has so far cost more than it would save in direct labor costs. The equipment needed to achieve an automated production system is very expensive. According to one estimate the average new equipment purchase needed to reduce labor requirements by one man-year is approximately $35,000.[11] Deterrents, similar to those found in the automobile industry, to the development of completely automatic systems can be found today in the steel, rubber, textiles, aircraft, machinery, and most other major industries.

In general, it appears that automation has not affected the composition of the labor force to the extent anticipated a decade ago and that the completely automatic factory or office may be a long way off in many American industries. However, this does not mean that there have been no problems resulting from the advent of automation or that there will be no serious problems in the future. The report of the National Commission on Technology, Automation, and Economic Progress, a seven-volume work published in 1966, contains the following statement regarding the current pace of technological change:

It has become almost a commonplace that the world is experiencing a scientific and technological revolution. Stock phrases—knowledge explosion, second industrial revolution, automation revolution—express this belief. According to one extreme view, the world—or at least the United States—is on the verge of a glut of productivity sufficient to make our economic institutions and the notion of gainful employment obsolete. We dissent from this view. We believe that the evidence does not support it, and that it diverts attention from the real problems of our country and the world. However, we also dissent from the other extreme view of complacency that denies the existence of serious social and economic problems related to the impact of technological change.[12]

This more balanced point of view regarding the effects of automation, which has emerged as the dominant one in the middle of the 1960s, is essentially the position taken in this chapter. If the rate of technological development as measured by productivity growth is not overwhelming, it is still substantial. The rate of change in the occupational composition of the labor force may not be accelerating, but the present rate imposes some important strains upon the institutions responsible for adjusting labor supply to labor demand. Although more than half of the labor force may be in industries that are not at all affected by automation, the figures reported above indicate that 17.2 percent, or approximately 12.1 million persons, were employed in 1964 in industries that are already at some stage of automation or are clearly moving in that direction. The view that we need not be concerned about automation either because it is not new or because it is not being introduced at the rate anticipated earlier rests upon the assumption that the adjustments we are currently making to technological change are adequate. This assumption does not appear to be warranted.

The possibility that there may be a further acceleration of the rate of technological development should also be considered. The technical problems that slow down the rate of introduction of automation today will not necessarily continue to do so in the future. Technological change does not occur in a smooth, unbroken sequence but rather in spurts of development. The gradual accumulation of minor improvements in processing and materials-handling techniques may eventually make it possible to move rapidly toward the complete integration of production processes around automatic controls in many more industries.

The report of the National Commission on Technology, Automation, and Economic Progress concludes that, "Past trends and current prospects suggest that the present is, and the near future will be, a time of rapid technological progress."[13] One important reason that this may be so is the substantially greater amounts being spent on research and development by both government and private industry. Total expenditures for research and development in the United States increased from $1.5 billion in 1945 to an estimated $17.4 billion in 1963.[14] Much of this change has come in recent years, with more than a 300 percent increase in research and development expenditures in the past decade. Almost two-thirds of the money used for this purpose has been spent by the Federal government, and over half of these government expenditures were made by the Department of Defense. Many of the results of research and development for the Armed Forces, however, have turned out to be immediately applicable in private industry—notable examples being the electronic computer, radar, jet aircraft, and microwave communication. Also, the expenditures by private industry on research with industrial rather than consumer applications represent a considerable sum of money and have been increasing at a rapid rate. The instruments, electrical equipment, and machinery industries, each of which is involved in the production of automation equipment, rank near the top among all industries in company-financed research and development activities.

Additional evidence of the increasing use of science by American industry is the growing number of scientists and engineers employed in research and development. In the decade 1951–1961, the number of research scientists and engineers grew from 158,000 to approximately 387,000.[15] The effects of increasing expenditures on research and increasing involvement of scientists and engineers in this process can be seen in the number of patents issued. In the five-year period from 1951 to 1955, 379,000 patents were issued, and in the period between 1960 and 1964, 457,000 were issued.[16] In contrast to earlier periods when most patent holders were individual inventors, patents today are granted, for the most part, to large corporations that employ the inventors in their laboratories. This rationalization of the invention process has also contributed to the accelerating rate of technological change.

An effort of this magnitude to develop new products and new production processes can almost certainly be expected to increase the rate at which automation is adopted in American industry. Some indication of the changing rate of adoption of new products and processes can be seen in the decreasing lapsed time between an invention and the recognition of its commercial potential: This averaged thirty years for innovations introduced between 1880 and 1919 and only nine years for those since World War II. One of these post-World War II developments was the computer; and in spite of the fact that it was introduced at a rapid rate almost from the beginning, in 1962 there were orders from United States manufacturers for more computer systems than had been built altogether since the first commercial computer was marketed in 1946.[17] Further evidence of the rate of increase in computer use is the fact that the 2,451 computers installed in Federal government agencies by mid-1966 represented an 85 percent increase over the number of computers (1,326) installed by mid-1963.[18]

The best strategy in all contemporary industrial societies, in view of their history of accelerating technological change and the current effort to stimulate new developments in production techniques, would appear to be to assume that the age of automation will come sooner than we think and to try to anticipate the problems that may be created by its arrival. John Diebold, president of a consulting firm specializing in the use of computer systems, has written the following about the advent of automation:

The first industrial revolution was a revolution not because of the new machines that were developed but because of the sweeping alterations they created in the social body. Society was completely and irrevocably changed, and the role of business within society was completely changed. The same thing is happening again, it is happening more rapidly, and the effects of the technological revolution we are now living through will run even deeper. We must identify the issue and prepare to meet it, or social change will engulf us.[19]

### Automation and Unemployment

The consequence of automation that has stimulated by far the greatest amount of public concern is the possibility that it may increase unemployment. Extensive congressional hearings have been held on the topic; and thousands of pages of newspapers, magazines, and books have been devoted to discussions of the issue. Concern with technological unemployment is, of course, not a new phenomenon. The Luddites, a group of early nineteenth-century English workmen, destroyed labor-saving machinery as a protest against threatened unemployment; and in one instance, a mob of workers drowned the inventor of a new machine. Contemporary concern with the employment effects of technological change seems to have focused almost exclusively upon automation. We shall attempt to assess the extent to which this concern is warranted.

An important thing to keep in mind throughout this discussion is that change in production technology is only one of a large number of interrelated factors affecting employment and unemployment levels. Population growth, government fiscal and monetary policies, international tensions, the composition of the labor force in terms of educational and skill levels, discriminatory hiring practices, government manpower programs, and public and private welfare systems would all have to be taken into account, along with technological change, in a full discussion of employment problems. The three major categories of factors affecting employment and unemployment rates are level of aggregate demand for goods and services, size and composition of the labor force, and productivity or level of output per man-hour of work. The nature of production technology is the major determinant of the level of productivity. Although technological change is therefore an important factor affecting the rate of unemployment, the emphasis it is given in this chapter should not be interpreted as meaning that it is the only one.

One line of argument regarding the potential effect of automation upon the level of unemployment is that change in production technology has in the past always resulted in *increased* long-run employment opportunities. The assumption here is that increased productivity permits lower prices, which stimulates economic growth and creates new industries and new jobs. Some popular writers, basing their contentions upon this assumption, have even predicted that the consequence of automation will be a long-run labor shortage. Other writers, while admitting that increased employment has accompanied technological change in the past, contend that there is no guarantee that it will do so in the future. They refer to the broad potential for application of automation and the generally accelerating rate of change, and they cite dramatic examples of increased productivity and decreased labor needs resulting from automation.

Throughout the 1950s a pattern seemed to have been established that lent strength to the argument that technological change was having an important effect upon unemployment levels. Periods of economic expansion following recessions stopped short of full recovery, and the unemployment rate became progressively higher at each peak of economic activity. Unemployed workers, and particularly the increasing number who were unemployed for long periods of time, were predominantly unskilled and uneducated; and the idea that increasing unemployment rates were the result of a technologically induced permanent reduction in the demand for such workers seemed a particularly plausible one. However there had been, at the time this chapter was written, an unprecedented six consecutive years of economic growth beginning in 1961, during which time the unemployment rate fell from 6.8 to 4 percent. The industrial and occupational pattern of this employment increase was as significant as its size. The average annual increase in employment in blue-collar occupations (2.9 percent) from 1961 to 1966 was actually higher than the annual average for white-collar occupations (2.0 percent). The largest percentage decreases in unemployment occurred among workers at the least skilled levels—the laborers and operatives. The experience of the past six years would seem to indicate that a sufficiently prolonged period of high aggregate consumer demand can still offset the effects upon employment of productivity increases resulting from technological development.

It should be noted that reducing the overall level of unemployment to 4 percent and making inroads upon the long-term unemployment of the unskilled required, in duration and total growth, the "outstanding peacetime performance of the U.S. economy in over half a century of record keeping."[20] Taking account of productivity changes, declining hours of work, and the increasing rate of growth in the size of the labor force, the National Commission on Technology, Automation, and Economic Progress arrived at the following conclusion regarding the necessary rate of economic growth: ". . . The output of the economy—and the aggregate demand to buy it—must grow in excess of 4 percent a year just to prevent the unemployment rate from rising, and even faster if the unemployment rate is to fall further, as we believe it should. Yet our economy has seldom, if ever, grown at a rate faster than 3.5 percent for any extended length of time. We have no cause for complacency."[21] It is clear that automation is having, and will continue to have, an effect upon the structure of demand for labor. Whether the demand for professionals, technicians, and other highly skilled workers will exceed the supply and whether the supply of unskilled workers will exceed demand, however, remains a moot point.

Differences of opinion about the long-run effect of automation upon employment cannot be resolved at our present state of knowledge. We simply do not know enough about the consequences of automation to make accurate forecasts over any long period of time. We can, however, predict with considerable confidence that there will be short-term dislocation of workers. Whatever its lesson regarding general employment levels in the long run, the history of change in production technology is replete with instances of displacement of workers by machines, and the experience with automation already suggests that it will not be an exception to this pattern. For the sixty-year-old semiskilled worker whose job is automated out of existence and who cannot qualify for new jobs such as computer programmer or automation engineer, Lord Keynes's famous comment that "in the long-run we are all dead" may be an especially poignant truth. There is almost universal recognition among industrial managers, trade-union leaders, and government manpower specialists that automation will displace some workers; and all three groups are engaged in developing procedures for cushioning this type of effect.

Most case studies of the introduction of automation indicate that, while there is technological *displacement* of workers, there has been relatively little *disemployment*. Workers whose jobs have been eliminated are frequently transferred to other jobs within the company. In some cases these transfers result in underemployment in the sense that the worker is being paid less, is not using skills he had acquired, or is working short shifts. Although there are human problems involved in the necessity for changing jobs and in underemployment, they are clearly less severe than those accompanying unemployment. Dire predictions of mass layoffs resulting from automation were often made during the 1950s when the automation of durable-goods industries was occurring at a more rapid rate. There have, in fact, been almost no cases of large-scale layoffs of workers from factories in these industries that could be traced directly to automation. The rapidly increasing use of computers in offices has likewise resulted in relatively little disemployment of clerical workers. Displacement or dislocation of some of these workers commonly accompanies the introduction of an electronic data-processing system, but transfers to new jobs and a high level of normal attrition through quits and retirements have made it possible to adjust to decreased manpower requirements without mass layoffs.

There is another set of factors which also has a bearing on the employment effect of automation so far. As was noted above, most of the current installations of computers, numerically controlled machines, feedback devices, or in-line transfer equipment do not represent true automation but are merely steps in that direction. They do not result in the complete integration of production processes but are designed instead to perform certain specific and limited functions. Very often these functions are ones that could not be performed using conventional equipment and include, for example, the production of a new product, improvements in an existing product, or the processing of information that was previously unavailable. Companies that are adding to their product line or improving the quality of old products, that need more rapid and efficient information-processing techniques, and that can afford expensive automated equipment to perform these functions are generally companies with an expanding demand for their products or services. In growing companies it is easier to absorb workers displaced by technological change from one part of the operation into other parts. To the extent that automated equipment is introduced primarily into expanding firms in order to do things that were not previously being done, the probability of extensive disemployment resulting from automation is slim.

The fact that relatively few industries have reached the advanced stages of automation is another important reason why it has so far been possible to absorb most technologically displaced workers into other jobs in the same firm. In contrast to automation, the process of mechanization (especially developments in processing operations) generally produces an occupational structure composed of many jobs at approximately the same skill level. The learning time on functionally specialized, semiskilled jobs is short, and the skills that exist are transferable from one job to another. A worker whose job is eliminated by mechanization can move with relative ease to another job in the same plant. As industries move closer to automation, the number of alternative possibilities for employment at the same skill level declines. There are fewer jobs within the firm to which the technologically displaced worker can be shifted, and the skills required may be less transferable. If many more industries make the transition from advanced mechanization to the beginning stage of automation, disemployment may become a more common consequence of technological change.

To say that automation has not yet produced mass layoffs is not the same thing as saying that it has not contributed to unemployment. The major employment effect of automation has not been upon the workers who are already in industry, many of whom are protected by seniority provisions and other job-security agreements, but upon the new entrants into the labor force who are not hired. Technological changes have clearly decreased the demand for young unskilled workers who are entering the labor market for the first time. The high school dropout is especially likely to experience increasing difficulty in finding and holding a job. Table 6 compares the unemployment rate for the sixteen-to-nineteen-year-old age group with unemployment in the total labor force from 1947 through 1965. There has been a clear and disproportionately high rate of increase of unemployment of teen-agers during the period covered in this table. The proportion of the unemployed who are teen-agers has risen steadily in recent years, and the average for the period from 1957 through 1965 is appreciably higher than the average for the preceding ten years. This pattern can be seen in the ratio of teen-age unemployment to total unemployment in Table 6.

Aggregating the unemployment figures for the sixteen-to-nineteen-year-old members of the labor force obscures the fact that some segments of this group had much higher rates than others. Table 7 compares the unemployment rate of high school graduates and school dropouts. The dropout obviously has a more difficult time finding

TABLE 6. Teen-age Unemployment Rates and Total
Unemployment Rates, 1947–1965

| Year | Total, 14 years and over | Ages 16–19 | Ratio of ages 16–19 to total |
|------|--------------------------|------------|------------------------------|
| 1947 | 3.9 | 9.6 | 2.5 |
| 1948 | 3.8 | 9.2 | 2.4 |
| 1949 | 5.9 | 13.4 | 2.3 |
| 1950 | 5.3 | 12.2 | 2.3 |
| 1951 | 3.3 | 8.2 | 2.5 |
| 1952 | 3.1 | 8.5 | 2.7 |
| 1953 | 2.9 | 7.6 | 2.6 |
| 1954 | 5.6 | 12.6 | 2.3 |
| 1955 | 4.4 | 11.0 | 2.5 |
| 1956 | 4.2 | 11.1 | 2.6 |
| 1957 | 4.3 | 11.6 | 2.7 |
| 1958 | 6.8 | 15.9 | 2.3 |
| 1959 | 5.5 | 14.6 | 2.7 |
| 1960 | 5.6 | 14.7 | 2.6 |
| 1961 | 6.7 | 16.8 | 2.5 |
| 1962 | 5.6 | 14.6 | 2.6 |
| 1963 | 5.7 | 17.2 | 3.0 |
| 1964 | 5.2 | 16.2 | 3.1 |
| 1965 | 4.6 | 14.8 | 3.2 |

SOURCE: *Manpower Report of the President,* March, 1966.

work than the high school graduate, and the amount of difficulty
he experiences appears to be increasing: Of those who quit school
any time during 1964 over one-third were still unemployed in October
of that year. Negro teen-agers also appear to be at an increasing
disadvantage in the job market. The percentage of all nonwhites
among the unemployed has remained constant or has declined in
recent years although their unemployment rate is still approximately
twice that of whites. The ratio of nonwhite *teen-age* unemployment
to total unemployment, however, has increased considerably in recent
years, which means that nonwhite teen-agers represent an increasingly larger percent of all unemployed persons. In 1965 the unemployment rate for nonwhite teen-agers was over twice that for white
teen-agers and was five and a half times the total unemployment
rate. The pattern of change in white and nonwhite teen-age unemployment is shown in Table 8.

**TABLE 7.  Unemployment of High School Graduates and Dropouts***

| Year | Total, 14 years and over Percent unemployed | High school graduates Percent unemployed | Ratio of graduates to total | School dropouts Percent unemployed | Ratio of dropouts to total |
|------|------|------|------|------|------|
| 1960 | 5.6 | 15.2 | 2.7 | 18.2 | 3.3 |
| 1961 | 6.7 | 17.9 | 2.7 | 26.8 | 4.0 |
| 1962 | 5.6 | 14.1 | 2.5 | 28.6 | 5.1 |
| 1963 | 5.7 | 18.0 | 3.2 | 31.7 | 5.6 |
| 1964 | 5.2 | 18.7 | 3.6 | 33.6 | 6.5 |

* Unemployment rates are for sixteen to twenty-four year old high school graduates not enrolled in colleges and of school dropouts as of October of year of graduation or dropout.
SOURCE: *Manpower Report of the President,* March, 1966.

**TABLE 8.  Unemployment of White and Nonwhite Teen-agers Fourteen to Nineteen Years Old, 1954–1965**

| Year | Total, 14 years and over Percent unemployed | White teen-agers Percent unemployed | Ratio of whites to total | Nonwhite teen-agers Percent unemployed | Ratio of nonwhites to total |
|------|------|------|------|------|------|
| 1954 | 5.6 | 10.9 | 2.0 | 14.7 | 2.6 |
| 1955 | 4.4 | 9.6 | 2.2 | 14.8 | 3.4 |
| 1956 | 4.2 | 9.5 | 2.3 | 17.4 | 4.1 |
| 1957 | 4.3 | 9.9 | 2.3 | 18.0 | 4.2 |
| 1958 | 6.8 | 13.0 | 1.9 | 25.0 | 3.8 |
| 1959 | 5.5 | 11.9 | 2.2 | 23.5 | 4.3 |
| 1960 | 5.6 | 12.4 | 2.2 | 22.1 | 4.0 |
| 1961 | 6.7 | 13.8 | 2.1 | 25.4 | 3.8 |
| 1962 | 5.6 | 12.0 | 2.1 | 23.7 | 4.2 |
| 1963 | 5.7 | 14.0 | 2.5 | 28.4 | 5.0 |
| 1964 | 5.2 | 13.3 | 2.6 | 26.2 | 5.0 |
| 1965 | 4.6 | 12.2 | 2.7 | 25.3 | 5.5 |

SOURCE: *Manpower Report of the President,* March, 1966.

As high as the figures in Tables 7 and 8 are, they undoubtedly understate the total amount of unemployment among teen-age school dropouts and Negroes. The unemployment rate represents the percent of persons who did not have a job and were looking for work during the week preceding the Department of Labor survey. People in segments of the population having particularly high unemployment rates are likely to become discouraged and drop out of the labor force in the sense that they are no longer looking for work—although they would accept it if it were available. This "hidden" unemployment is especially high among the unskilled and uneducated.[22] For the teen-age Negro school dropout, faced with discrimination based upon both age and race and hampered by the lack of any marketable skill, the prospect of finding employment must appear remote; and the real unemployment rate is probably much higher than that shown in the official reports. In a period of unprecedented prosperity, the combination of a high unemployment rate among Negro teen-agers and their concentration in urban ghettos is an explosive condition that is clearly involved in the rioting which has occurred in many cities.

The employment problems of teen-agers are, of course, not entirely a consequence of automation. If this were so, we would expect the unemployment rate among semiskilled operatives and unskilled laborers—jobs through which many teen-agers enter the labor force—to have increased. Although these occupational categories represent a declining percentage of the total labor force, the absolute number of people in such jobs is still increasing and the proportion of all unemployed persons who are laborers or machine operators has actually decreased in recent years. Probably the most important single factor accounting for the high unemployment rate among teen-agers is the record number of young people currently entering the labor force. Because of the increase in the birthrate in the period following World War II, the Department of Labor estimates that there will be 40 percent more new entrants into the labor force during the 1960s than in the preceding decade. The increasing number of people who have high school diplomas aggravates the problem of the dropout, since he is competing for jobs with more and better-educated young men and women. Even with the continuing increase in the proportion of people who finish high school, dropouts still constitute a very large percentage of young workers. In a study conducted in February,

1963, 45 percent of the sixteen-to-twenty-one-year-old youth out of school had not completed high school.[23] The accelerating rate of technological change along with the dramatic increase in the number of new entrants into the labor force, many of whom will be school dropouts, means that the problem of teen-age unemployment is likely to become worse. Although the overall level of unemployment declined in 1966 to 4 percent, the composition of the unemployed appears to be changing, with young people representing an increasing proportion—one-third of all jobless workers in 1965 were between the ages of sixteen and twenty-one. The economy is not generating enough jobs for new unskilled entrants into the labor force; and although automation is not the only cause, it is clearly a contributing factor. The 1966 *Manpower Report of the President* describes the problems that complicate job finding for disadvantaged youth:

The most rapid growth in employment will tend to be in occupations requiring high school education or above, for which large numbers of disadvantaged youth cannot qualify. Opportunities in lower level jobs are expected to be much more limited.

Employment on farms will continue to decline, leading to a further rural-to-urban population shift. This will move more poorly educated youth, including many nonwhites, into cities, where they have no easy means of entry into employment and where they must compete with young people who have had better educational opportunities.

Partly because of this farm-to-city migration, it will be difficult to eradicate city slums, where poor, uneducated families cluster, all too often transmitting to their children a pattern of lack of education, low-paid and irregular work, frustration and failure.[24]

What may be said in summary about employment problems related to automation? First it should be noted that, at our present state of knowledge, it is impossible to precisely calculate the effects of technological change upon unemployment rates, particularly in the long run. It would be safe to say, however, that these effects have not been nearly so dire as predictions a decade ago would have led us to expect. A high and sustained growth in consumer demand can still offset the effects of productivity change at the current rate.[25]

Optimism regarding this fact, however, should be tempered by the recognition that an exceptionally high rate of economic growth will need to be maintained to prevent an increase in the level of unemployment at the present rate of growth in productivity. Furthermore, the probability that technological change will accelerate productivity growth must also be taken into account. Regardless of the effect of automation upon the overall rate of unemployment, it will undoubtedly cause temporary displacement of some additional workers; and both private and public retraining programs and other procedures designed to facilitate the movement of these workers from their present jobs to new jobs will need to be expanded. The major employment effect of automation now appears to be—and probably will continue to be—upon the new entrant into the labor force rather than upon those already employed. Job opportunities for school dropouts will almost certainly decline, and much more effort in manpower programs will need to be directed to the employment problems of young workers. Improvement in both the quality and the quantity of vocational counseling, including an increased effort to prevent students from dropping out of school, should be an important part of such programs. Many schools now have no vocational counselors; those that do are chiefly high schools, and dropouts often leave school without having received any counseling at all. Most people now drift into occupations rather than planning for, and making a choice among, a number of available alternatives. The pace at which change in the world of work is occurring may soon require, if it does not already, a more rational process of vocational choice.

Although the employment and unemployment effects of automation have generated by far the greatest amount of public concern, the issues related to automation and to rapid technological change generally are not limited to these effects. One such issue, the characteristics of work in automated plants and offices, will be considered in Chapter 3. The remainder of this chapter will be concerned with one of the probable effects of automation that may be felt outside the work place. In the long run, the most revolutionary consequence of automation may be its potential for reducing hours of work.

## Automation and Leisure

Twentieth-century Western civilization is confronted by at least one problem unique in human history. Man's historical preoccupation—working for the means of livelihood—is involving a diminishing portion of his time and energy. The problem of extracting from the earth the means of subsistence in an economy of scarcity has been replaced by a new set of problems in an economy of machine-made abundance. One such problem is the proper utilization of larger and larger amounts of available leisure time.

Many societies in the past have supported leisure classes of varying sizes with varying amounts of time free from productive activities. Leisure today is no longer the privilege of the few, however, but the prerogative of many. Never before has the question of how leisure time is to be used assumed such importance. Concern with the possibility that it might be misused is, however, not at all new. Shibboleths such as "the devil makes work for idle hands" are of ancient origin. Opponents of the English Ten Hours Bill, prior to its enactment in 1847, argued that decreasing hours of work would lead to the moral degeneration of workers. Similar outcries were heard in 1926 when the Ford Motor Company inaugurated the five-day week. At that time a chamber of commerce president in a large American city said that "mankind does not thrive on holidays—idle hours breed mischief"; a president of a major corporation was also quoted as saying that "it [the five-day week] would mean a trend toward the arena—Rome did that, and Rome died."[26]

In 1966 a cotton mill in Leigh, England, began a shift system involving a *three-day week* at full pay. The workers are divided into two teams, each of which works at 10½-hour shift on three days. One team works Sunday, Monday, and Tuesday nights and then has the next seven days off before working Wednesday, Thursday, and Friday. This reduction in the work week was possible because expensive new machinery in the plant could be kept in operation for more hours each week and output was increased. A newspaper account of this development contained the following description of a problem it produced:

The cotton workers of this town of 50,000 are totally unprepared for the increased leisure time. It's not so bad for the married men but the single lads are grumbling.

"It used to be a struggle to make ends meet," said Cliff Porter. Now my wife goes to work while I do the housework and cook for my daughters. All the wife has to do when she gets home is put her feet up!"

Peter Taylor, a 30-year-old bachelor, sees it differently. "It was a marvelous experience to begin with. There was plenty of time for fishing and general relaxation. But now I'm just bored, waiting for my friends to finish work. I've tried gardening, decorating, going to the cinema, but it's becoming a drag."

A three-day work week may be a rarity for some time to come. There seems to be little doubt, however, that there will be a continuing decline in the number of hours worked; and the four-day week may be feasible throughout the nonfarm sector of our economy in the next twenty years.[27] The number of hours and days worked per week during any period tends to be regarded as natural and immutable. The five-day, forty-hour work week is currently so regarded. However, it has only been a decade or so that this amount of working time has been the standard work week in this country. In the past century the average number of hours worked per week by nonagricultural workers has decreased from about sixty-five to about forty hours, and this decline has been fairly steady, averaging about three hours per decade. It is the process of reduction of working time which appears to be "natural and immutable."

The increasing productivity of our economy is what has made this reduction in working hours possible. For the economy as a whole, output per man-hour has been rising by 2 to 3 percent per year over the past fifty years. In the nongovernmental sector of our economy, output per man-hour has approximately doubled over the past twenty-five years. The benefits of this increased productivity have been distributed between income and leisure on roughly a 60–40 basis, 60 percent going into greater income and 40 percent for more leisure time.[28] Whether this particular way of cutting the "productivity pie" will continue or not is difficult to predict. Some of the factors affecting the likelihood that automation will produce a further increase in available leisure time may be considered.

The most important reason for expecting a further decline in working hours is the likelihood, discussed above, of a continuation and perhaps an acceleration of the growth of productivity. The extent to which this increased productivity will be translated into shorter hours of work will probably be determined in part by the amount of pressure brought to bear by trade unions and labor generally for reduced hours. The logic of cost reduction would, in most instances, dictate a management preference for longer hours and fewer workers when the point is reached at which a decrease in hours worked no longer increases productivity. This may be especially true where there are pressures to maintain continuous operation of expensive automated equipment in order to meet amortization deadlines. Thus far, a further reduction in the work week has not become an immediate collective-bargaining objective of American trade unions generally. However, a number of unions, including the large pattern-setting UAW, are committed to the shorter week as a long-term collective-bargaining goal; and it seems probable that, with continued productivity increases, union pressure for decreased hours in other industries will follow.

Since the various industries within our economy are differentially susceptible to further mechanization, the possibility for decreasing hours of work may vary from industry to industry. Reductions in hours worked per week have occurred at varying rates in different industries in the past and will undoubtedly continue to do so. Because of the rate of change in production techniques and the likelihood that there will be greater pressure exerted to reduce the work week, it is probable that working hours of employees in mass-production industries will be among the first to be affected by automation. Hours of work are now declining faster for manual workers than for professional or managerial workers. In industries such as retail trade where productivity is increasing very slowly, the five-day work week did not become widespread until after World War II. The general, long-run mechanism through which hours of work are reduced, even in occupations or industries in which productivity growth does not warrant it, is the shift of an increasing percentage of the labor force into these occupations and industries so that the work can be divided among more people who work fewer hours.

Relatively greater pressure to decrease the work week for production-line workers may develop first for a number of reasons. Automation appears to have already decreased the number of job opportunities available to such workers in some industries and, barring any great increases in product demand, seems likely to do so in others. To the extent that automation results in reduced job opportunities, even in the absence of large-scale displacement of workers, it is likely that there will be pressure exerted by many unions to decrease hours in order to spread available jobs among a larger number of people.

Changing standards regarding adequacy of style of life among working-class families may also affect preferences regarding the distribution of income and leisure from increased productivity. Amount of income desired tends to be normatively regulated; and there is some evidence that once a standard of living is established, there may be less pressure to raise income than to maintain it at a customary level.[29] Demands for new goods and services are constantly being created by advertising campaigns and, more subtly, through models provided by the mass media; the consumption of many of these goods and services is dependent upon *both* greater income and more leisure. Many leisure activities which were once symbols of upper-class status are now within the means of working-class families, and it is unlikely that the demand for more leisure time in which to enjoy these activities will slacken.

In a study in the automobile industry in 1957, a sample of workers from an automated plant were asked whether they would prefer a shorter work week, increased wages, or longer vacations if any of these alternatives were made possible by automation. Almost three-fourths indicated a preference for a shorter work week over either more pay or longer vacations. One apparent reason for this preference is the very nature of production-line work. Jobs of this kind have characteristically required little exercise of skill, responsibility, or initiative and have offered little variety in the types of tasks performed. At least in its early stage, automation does not appear to have significantly altered these characteristics of production-line work. If work is not a satisfying experience, it would seem reasonable to expect that there would be greater pressure to decrease working hours to allow more time for what may be perceived as more important and more satisfying activities. The meaning and relative importance of work and leisure activities will be considered in more detail in Chapter 3, where the factors producing alienation from work will be discussed.

There has not yet been sufficient research dealing with the factors affecting the preference of workers for greater leisure or more income to accurately anticipate the preferred distribution of the benefits of increased productivity from automation. It seems likely, however, that increasing productivity will continue to result in an increase in available leisure time. If a change of this type does occur, the nature of leisure activities may be affected. There is evidence from previous research that the proportion of time spent in various activities increases or decreases depending upon the amount of leisure time available.[30]

A number of dimensions of leisure activities may be considered in discussing the use of leisure time. Leisure may be recuperative in the sense that time is spent relaxing from the job completed and preparing for the job forthcoming, or it may be actively spent in the sense of physical or emotional involvement in an activity. Leisure time may be used creatively or noncreatively. It may be self-oriented or may be other- or service-oriented. It may be spent in the company of others or in solitary pursuits. It may be spent as a spectator of, or as a participant in, various activities. Leisure time may serve as relief from boredom or as escape from involvement.

Automation may affect patterns of use of leisure time either by increasing the amount of time available for such activities or by changing the nature of the work experience. The combination of decreased physical effort required by automated jobs and decreased working hours would make possible a decrease in the proportion of time spent in recuperation from work and permit more active involvement in leisure pursuits. Since recuperative time is likely to be noncreative, there would be at least the possibility for more creative use of leisure with increased time available. Production-line workers desiring creative outlets would necessarily seek such experience in leisure activities because of the essentially noncreative character of work in either automated or conventional plants. Passive recuperative time being primarily self-oriented, there would also be the possibility of an increase in service-oriented activities given more leisure time.

One of the effects of automation upon some types of production-line jobs has been the social isolation of workers because of increased distance between work stations and increased attention required by the job.[31] Social isolation on the job may result in a larger proportion of leisure time spent in activities involving others. This may be especially true for production-line workers, whose occupational roles do not encourage "self-esteem testing" on the job so that recognition of success is more likely to be sought in leisure activities. For this reason it is also likely that, given sufficient time to acquire skills adequate to ensure some measure of success in these activities, workers may spend a larger proportion of leisure time as participants in activities rather than as spectators.[32] Finally, it follows from the preceding discussion of the relation of work and leisure that for production-line workers, leisure activities are more apt to function as relief from boredom than escape from involvement. For any occupational group in which work is seen as a means rather than an end in itself, leisure is less likely to represent freedom from involvement than it is freedom to become involved.

The opportunity to engage in more and different leisure pursuits is, of course, no guarantee that increased leisure time will be effectively used. David Riesman has commented that "for many people today, the sudden onrush of leisure is a version of technological unemployment: their education has not prepared them for it and the creation of new wants at their expense moves faster than their ability to order and assimilate these wants."[33] The question of what constitutes effective use of leisure time is not easily answered. Time spent fishing or watching television is not inherently better or worse than time spent reading or engaging in volunteer community service. With greater amounts of time available, it seems likely that a varied pattern of activities, balanced along the dimensions of use of leisure described above, would provide a more satisfying set of experiences. Factors that have been repeatedly identified as determinants of job satisfaction—such as variety of tasks performed, amount of responsibility involved, level of skill required, quality of interpersonal relations, recognition for achievement, and opportunity for creativity and self-expression—would undoubtedly also affect satisfaction with leisure. Whereas these aspects of the job are fixed for most people by the nature of their occupational role, the responsibility for building them into leisure pursuits is largely left to the individual. Constructing a satisfying pattern of leisure experiences requires a set of interests and skills that most people in industrial societies have not yet acquired.

A second way of looking at what constitutes effective use of leisure is in terms of the needs of the community or society. There are a great many opportunities for engaging in volunteer service activities for political parties, hospitals, welfare agencies, recreation programs, youth organizations, and local government. And these volunteer activities are perennially understaffed. Another example, and probably a more important one, of a way in which increased leisure could serve the needs of industrial societies would be the opportunity it might provide for developing a better-informed public. Time spent in acquiring information about current events through adult education courses or general reading would certainly be time well spent in view of the demands placed upon the electorate in rapidly changing industrial societies. Public-opinion polls have repeatedly demonstrated that a substantial proportion of our population is ill-informed about, or even unaware of, many important public issues. An effective democratic system under conditions of rapid social change requires a well-informed electorate.

The most appropriate place for training in the use of leisure time would seem to be the public schools. Although there is already a growing emphasis in American education upon training for citizenship in the community and a deemphasis of vocational training, it may be important for curriculum planners to recognize that the citizen in the automated industrial community may have a large amount of leisure time at his disposal. Automation may require that more adequate provision be made for training in certain kinds of technical skills as well. But in the long run, the primary responsibility of the schools may well become that of instilling certain kinds of values and interests which permit the effective use of leisure and, in general, teaching not vocational but leisure skills.

The inadequacy of our institutionalized or rationalized procedures for training in the use of leisure time is not the only way in which industrial societies are ill-prepared for a rapid increase in the amount of available leisure. Recreational facilities in most communities are, for example, clearly inadequate for our present needs without any further decrease in working hours. There is, however, widespread recognition of the necessity for providing more parks, playgrounds, swimming pools, and other outdoor and indoor recreational facilities in urban areas. Many major cities, New York City is one example, have extensive and imaginative plans for developing more and better recreational opportunities. A more difficult problem is the conservation of natural resources and preservation of wilderness areas under the pressure of population growth, easier access through improved highway systems, and increased time free for travel. The dilemma can be seen in a bill recently introduced in Congress which recommended that an area in the Midwest be set aside as a wilderness area, but described it as being able to accommodate *a million annual visitors*. We are rapidly destroying the very things that have traditionally drawn us to the out-of-doors. Senator Gaylord Nelson of Wisconsin recently suggested that America's countryside is now suffering the same fate as its cities and described the problem as follows: "Our rivers and lakes are clogging up with sewage, chemicals, and refuse. Irreplaceable scenic lakeshores and marshes have been converted to cottage subdivisions. Public parks and campgrounds are so overcrowded they are little more than outdoor slums. The roads to our tourist attractions are lined with garish billboards and carnival-type entertainment."[34]

The total number of visits to national parks in 1966 was approximately 117 million—33 percent more than the 88 million that had been predicted and planned for that year a decade ago. At one time there were almost two million acres of redwood forests in California.

Today there is only about 10 percent of this acreage, and the fight to preserve even a small portion of these forests in a Redwoods National Park had not yet been successful in 1966. Demand for hydroelectric power has resulted in proposals to place two dams in the Grand Canyon of the Colorado and another dam in the Yukon River that would flood a wilderness area in Alaska larger than the state of New Jersey. Only about 2.7 percent of the 3,700 miles of shore along the Atlantic-Gulf Coasts is now available for public use. The number of fishermen and hunters in the country has grown somewhat faster than the rate of population growth and very much faster than the rate of natural increase in the number of fish and game. Problems of this sort illustrate the fact that a major effort by conservationists will be necessary to prevent the destruction of our natural heritage under the pressure of demand for mass recreation and other types of land use. A further reduction in working hours for a substantial proportion of the population may make the problem an insoluble one.

## Summary

This chapter has focused upon the nature of automation, the rate at which it is occurring, its effect upon employment, and some consequences of the increasing leisure it may allow. This focus does not reflect a conviction that the effects of automation will be limited to these areas. The number of possible consequences of automation that might be discussed is limited only by the span of years considered and the scope of one's imagination. However, problems related to employment and number of hours worked are the most direct and immediate effects of increasing productivity from automation, and they are the problems that have generated the greatest amount of public concern. Considerable attention has been devoted in this chapter to the nature of automation and the rate at which it is being introduced because a better understanding of contemporary technological change may help to dispel some of the fears automation has engendered and because it is the *rate* of change in production technology that determines the severity of the problems it creates.

The advent of the age of automation appears to be neither as imminent nor as ominous as it was thought to have been a few years ago. There have been no mass layoffs directly attributable to automation; the overall level of unemployment still appears to respond adequately to a prolonged period of high consumer demand; the rate of change in the occupational composition of the labor force has, if anything, slowed down in recent years; and the pace at which automated equipment is being introduced into many major industries is much slower than had been anticipated. If automation represents a second industrial revolution, it is apparent that the revolution has not yet begun.

The major point, however, in our discussion of the nature of automation was that most of the technological advances that have been called automation are only steps in that direction. Whatever revolutionary consequences there may be are unlikely to be felt until industries employing a larger proportion of the labor force have achieved fully integrated and automatically controlled production systems. The enormous sums of money being spent on research and development suggest that production systems of this sort may become common in more industries in the near future. If the problems that may be caused by automation are not a present danger, they nevertheless require adjustments that should be anticipated and planned for at the present time.

Complacency regarding the probable effects of automation would be justified only if we were adequately adjusting to current technological changes and could anticipate that the rate of introduction and type of new production technology in the future would not differ from the present. Neither of these assumptions appears to be warranted. As examples of problems to which current technological change is a contributing factor, we have emphasized unemployment among teen-age entrants into the labor force and the inadequacy of individual and institutional preparation for the use of leisure time. These problems exist today and will undoubtedly become worse if automation becomes more widespread. It should be noted that these problems are treated here as *examples* of problems related to current technological change; discussion of the complete list of such problems would be beyond the scope of this book. And it should also be noted that automation is only *one example* of a direction in which production systems are evolving, although it is the one which is currently the center of attention.

In the broader context of the concerns of this book, problems related to automation, employment, and leisure are examples of difficulties created by rapid change, extensive structural differentiation, and lack of social integration. Coordination of labor supply and labor demand becomes a problem only in societies characterized by an elaborate and changing division of labor. Lack of such coordination may result in unemployment; but more important, though a less obvious problem, may be a failure to make the most effective use of the talents existing in the labor force. In the absence of rationalized procedures for occupational choice in industrial societies, realization of the productive potential of the labor force becomes less likely. At the very least, an improved program of vocational counseling in the schools—an instance of rationalization—should decrease the frequency of occupational *drift*, increase the frequency of occupational *choice*, and make it more likely that people will find jobs commensurate with their abilities. Rationalization of the process of occupational choice should decrease unemployment in addition to increasing productivity, and achieving both these objectives will become increasingly critical with any further acceleration in the rate of technological change.

Lack of preparation for leisure is also an example of a lag between the development of rationalized procedures for dealing with a problem and the emergence of the problem in the course of rapid social change. The conflict of interest between conservationists and recreationists referred to above is an example of another sort of problem— lack of social integration—that would be unlikely to occur in societies less complex and differentiated than our own. There are important conflicts of value that underlie many of the issues discussed in this chapter. If the rate of technological change begins to exceed our ability to adjust to it, to what extent should the introduction of new production techniques be controlled? What price in individual freedom of action would we be willing to pay in order to eliminate unemployment among teen-age Negroes in urban ghettos? Although it seems obvious that we are becoming an increasingly leisure-oriented society, it is not nearly so apparent that we *should* become so. The increased national product resulting from a continuation of the present pattern of working hours plus increased productivity could be used to improve a wide variety of services, such as public education, that are not now adequately financed. These and other value conflicts related to the general dilemma of freedom versus control will be discussed in Chapter 4. The intent of this chapter has been to illustrate problems occasioned by technological change that are unique to industrial societies. In Chapter 3 we shall consider another class of social problems inherent in the structure of industrial society—the alienation of the individual.

# 3

# ALIENATION IN INDUSTRIAL SOCIETY

The most persistent indictment of industrial society is that it has resulted in the alienation of industrial man. Loneliness in the midst of urban agglomeration; loss of social anchorage in mass society; the absence of a predictable life trajectory in an era of unprecedented social change; and the powerlessness of man within the complex social, economic, and political systems he has created are common themes in the social criticism of the industrial way of life. Concern with the alienated quality of existence is particularly widespread today since poverty, which was once the major target of social critics, has become less common. However, alienation has been recognized and condemned as a product of industrialism almost from the time of the initial disruption of traditional ways during the Industrial Revolution.

The increasing social isolation and estrangement of man has been noted by social philosophers from Kierkegaard to Cassirer, by novelists from Dostoyevsky to Camus, by poets from Yeats to Eliot, and by playwrights from Ibsen to Ionesco. Contemporary concern with alienation in industrial society is reflected in both the titles and the content of such recent works as David Riesman's *The Lonely Crowd*,

Robert Nisbet's *Quest for Community,* Erich Fromm's *Escape from Freedom,* and Karl Menninger's *Man against Himself.* The pervasiveness of alienation is suggested by the contention that the history of man is also the history of man's alienation—an idea expressed by both Hegel and Marx in the nineteenth century and by Erich Kahler in the middle of the twentieth.

## The Meaning of Alienation

In this chapter we shall consider the meaning of alienation, identify its roots in the social structure of industrial society, and discuss its consequences for industrial man. We shall begin with the conception of alienation that has had most effect upon the contemporary view of the process, that of Karl Marx. Particularly in his early writing, Marx was influenced by Hegel's idea that there is a "universal essence" of man which, as it is realized, constitutes the self-fulfillment of mankind. According to Marx, this process of self-fulfillment takes place only through productive or creative labor. He states that labor is the "existential activity of man, his free conscious activity—not a means for maintaining his life but for developing his universal nature."[1] It is through his labor that man should achieve the development of his full potentialities. With the mechanization of production under the capitalist system, however, the process of self-realization is frustrated, and the alienation of labor results. Erich Fromm, in *Marx's Concept of Man,* describes this view of alienation as follows:

> Alienation (or "estrangement") means, for Marx, that man does not experience himself as the acting agent in his grasp of the world, but that the world (nature, others, and he himself) remain alien to him. They stand above and against him as objects, even though they may be objects of his own creation. Alienation is essentially experiencing the world and oneself passively, receptively, as the subject separated from the object.[2]

According to Marx, alienation takes a number of forms. The laborer is, first of all, alienated from the product of his labor: He has no control over the disposition of the commodities he produces.

Regarding this type of alienation, Marx states that "the object which labor produces, its product, is encountered as an alien entity, a force that has become independent of its producer."[3]

Second, the worker is alienated from the means of production. With the advent of the factory system, the worker no longer owned the tools or the machinery with which he worked. Through the wage contract he sold his labor as a commodity; and because he no longer had control over his work life, his activity at work was estranged from the rest of his existence.

These two meanings of alienation have an anachronistic ring in the middle of the twentieth century. Laying aside for the moment metaphysical concerns with "human essence" and polemics regarding who *should* own the products of labor and the means of production, it is doubtful that many workers today *experience* these forms of alienation. To the extent that a sense of deprivation is the subjective counterpart of alienation, it seems unlikely that automobile workers feel alienated because they do not own either the assembly line or the completed automobiles that few even see leaving the assembly line. Concern with having some voice in decisions regarding work pace and conditions of employment, which is a real concern for workers today, is but a faint echo of Marx's call for ownership of the product and the means of production—a call, it should be added, that did have meaning to many workers in the eighteenth and nineteenth centuries.

These two forms of alienation have a more prominent place in Marx's later and more polemical writing. There is another type of alienation, however, that concerned Marx in both his *Economic and Philosophical Manuscripts*, written in 1844, and in *Capital*, which was written almost twenty-five years later. And this type of alienation is even more common today than when Marx first described it. This form of alienation has been labeled *self-estrangement*; it results from the fact that work no longer provides the opportunity for creative self-expression and, hence, alienates man from himself. Marx notes the "separation of the intellectual powers of production from manual labor" through the use of machine technology and suggests that the "special skill of each individual, insignificant factory operative vanishes as an infinitesimal quantity before science, the gigantic physical forces, and the mass of labor that are embodied in the factory mechanism."[4] In another context, Marx described this form of alienation as follows:

What constitutes alienation of labor? First, that work is *external* to the worker, that it is not part of his nature; and that, consequently, he does not fulfill himself in his work but denies himself, has a feeling of misery rather than well-being, does not develop freely his mental and physical energies but is physically exhausted and mentally debased. The worker therefore feels himself at home only during his leisure time, whereas at work he feels homeless. His work is not voluntary but imposed, *forced labor*. It is not the satisfaction of a need, but only a means for satisfying other needs.[5]

It is the fact that work is a means rather than an end—is an instrumental rather than a consummatory activity—that gives it its alien character. According to Marx, this form of alienation resulted not just from change in production technology but also from the advent of the capitalist economic system. From the vantage point of the present, it seems clear that the complex differentiated division of labor generated by industrial technology would produce alienation from work irrespective of the type of economic system in which it is embedded. Large-scale production and bureaucratization, along with the functionally specialized nature of jobs, have made it impossible for workers to feel that they have an active and important role in the production process or that their work is an end in itself. The sense of being a passive rather than an active agent is both a consequence of, and is made more tolerable by, the experience of an activity as merely instrumental, as a means to some more important end.

Marx regarded the working class as the most alienated class; consequently, his aim was the "emancipation of the workers." Fromm points out that, in the light of subsequent events, Marx's preoccupation with the alienated manual worker was misplaced—alienation has "become the fate of the vast majority of people."[6] Many white-collar workers today are more alienated than some manual workers,

especially skilled craftsmen, who may experience very little alienation from work. Fromm also contends that alienation is not limited
to the work place. He states that "alienation as we find it in modern
society is almost total; it pervades the relationship of man to his
work, to the things he consumes, to the state, to his fellow man, and
to himself."[7] Fromm, like Marx, emphasizes the passivity and powerlessness of man: ". . . [man] does not experience himself as the
center of his world, as the creator of his own acts—but his acts and
their consequences have become his masters . . . his actions are
not his own; while he is under the illusion of doing what *he* wants,
he is driven by forces which are separated from his self. . . ." And
in the same vein, "man does not experience himself as the active
bearer of his own powers and richness, but as an impoverished
'thing,' dependent on powers outside of himself. . . ."[8] Fromm has
written extensively on the subject of the alienation of industrial man,
and we shall refer again to his view of this process later in this
chapter.

The necessity for man, if he is to achieve self-fulfillment, to be
an active agent, to be both "the author and the actor of his history";
the importance of creative work in this process; and the extent to
which the contemporary industrial order involves work that can only
be experienced as a means to other ends—these are the themes from
Marx's view of alienation that we have selected for emphasis. They
have been selected not because they represent a comprehensive view
of Marx's treatment of the subject but because they are among those
of his observations that have stood the test of time and because they
serve to introduce the particular conception of alienation that will
be developed in this chapter. The term *alienation* has been used
in such a variety of ways that it comes close to being a shorthand
expression for all the socially based psychological maladies of modern
man. For this reason, it is important that we specify the meaning
of alienation that will be used in the discussion which follows.

Melvin Seeman has identified five alternative meanings of alienation that represent the major ways in which the concept has been
used in traditional sociological analysis.[9] The first and perhaps most
common of these usages is in terms of *powerlessness*. It is this type

of alienation with which Marx was primarily concerned in his analysis of the working class. As was noted above, however, loss of control over the important events that affect our lives has become an almost universal experience in complex mass societies. A second major usage of the term alienation may be labeled _meaninglessness_. Various writers have noted the increasing difficulty in rapidly changing segmented societies in finding appropriate standards for judgment regarding courses of action or patterns of belief. Meaninglessness refers, more specifically, to the difficulty in making accurate predictions about the behavior of others or about the outcome of our own actions. Situations have meaning to us to the extent that we are able to anticipate their outcome. Industrialism has increased the incidence of social situations that are meaningless in this sense. A third type of alienation, according to Seeman, is _normlessness_. This type is based upon Emile Durkheim's concept of _anomie_, which refers to a situation in which there are no effective norms or rules for behavior. As the term has been used in contemporary sociology, it has come to mean a circumstance in which there are no legitimate means to achieve socially prescribed goals. In industrial societies, for example, emphasis upon the goal of economic success is more pervasive than are the legitimate means for attaining this goal. The expectation that it is necessary to use socially unapproved means to be successful illustrates normlessness in Seeman's sense. _Isolation_ represents a fourth way in which the concept of alienation has been used. According to Seeman, "the alienated in the isolation sense are those who, like the intellectual, assign a low reward value to goals or beliefs that are typically highly valued in the given society."[10] The hippie who rejects prevailing middle-class values, the political extremist who advocates the destruction of current political institutions, and the hermit who completely renounces the contemporary way of life all share this form of alienation. The final variant of alienation found in sociological writing is _self-estrangement_. Both Marx and Fromm use the concept in this way. A person is self-estranged when he engages in activities that are not meaningful in themselves but are simply means to other ends. We can describe the person as being alienated from himself under these circumstances because what he is doing is not something that *he* regards as being important. "The worker who works only for his salary, the house-wife who cooks only to get it over with, or the other-directed type who acts 'only for its effect on others'—are instances of self-estrangement."[11]

Although these five types of alienation are conceptually independent, there are some ways in which they are linked. They may form a causal chain in which one or more types of alienation tend to produce another. The combination of powerlessness, meaninglessness, and normlessness is very likely to result in isolation: People who have little control over the factors that affect the achievement of a goal, who are unclear about what the goal should be, and who feel that whatever the goal is it cannot be achieved through approved means frequently respond by placing a low value upon achievement of that goal and are consequently alienated from a society in which it is typically highly valued.

Isolation, in the sense in which Seeman uses the term, refers to alienation from the total society. The same process may be seen at other levels as well. The worker who feels powerless and who sees the work place as meaningless and normless is unlikely to be very concerned with the goals of the work organization and is therefore isolated or alienated from it. An adolescent may feel alienated from his family for the same reasons.

A person who is isolated in the sense of having assigned a "low reward value to goals or beliefs that are typically highly valued" in any social situation is necessarily self-estranged in that situation. If we feel compelled to maintain membership in a group or organization whose goals we do not share, our activity in that group or organization will be perceived as a means to some other end. If we do not share the goals or values of the people with whom we associate, we are alienated not only from them but also from our "selves" to the extent that we minimize our investment of "self" in the situation, i.e., to the extent that we routinize our behavior and act in ways that bear little relationship to our image of the kind of person we think we are. The idea that we may be isolated from others and consequently alienated from our "selves" is the core of the conception of alienation that will be used in this chapter. It is a complex idea, however, and requires elaboration.

First of all, when we speak of alienation or estrangement, we need to specify what it is that the person is alienated or estranged *from*. Powerlessness, meaninglessness, and normlessness do not in themselves represent conditions of being alienated from some particular "thing," although they undoubtedly tend to produce such a condition. Second, no one is alienated from everything. The classic discussions of the topic by Marx, Weber, Durkheim, Fromm, Merton, and others have emphasized either alienation from other people (isolation) or alienation from the self (self-estrangement).

To say that a person is alienated from himself is only a figure of speech unless we have something specific in mind when we refer to the "self." In social psychological terms, the self is an organized set of ideas we hold about ourselves. If a person asks himself the question, "Who am I?" his answer would represent the "self" in this sense. Human beings have the capacity to be objects to themselves and consequently have attitudes, beliefs, and opinions about themselves just as they do about other things in their environment.

The conception of self is not a constant or fixed image but changes over time and changes as we move from one situation to another. The answer to the question, "Who am I?" would not be precisely the same when a person is at home with his family as when he is at the office with his colleagues.

One of the important things that change as we move from one situation to another is the set of criteria we use in evaluating our self. A different set of attributes is involved in being a good husband or father from that in being a good electrician or trade-union member. There may also be differences in the extent to which success in various social roles affects what a person thinks of himself. For some persons, being a success as a father may have a much greater effect upon self-esteem than being a success at work. For others the reverse may be true.

One's image of self in any role may or may not be an *evaluated* image. A person may think of himself as a "good student," a "bad student," or simply as a "student" without any evaluative connotation. Maintenance of self-esteem is a selective process in that we choose from among the roles that we play certain ones in which we need to succeed in order to think well of ourselves; in others we may fail without adverse effect upon self-esteem. Selection of one set of roles for self-evaluation rather than another also implies the selection of one set of evaluative criteria or "values" rather than another. The values we use in the process of attempting to maintain self-esteem represent the central values around which our personalities are structured. When we know what a person needs to do in order to think well of himself, we know a lot about that person.

A self-concept is not something with which we are born but something that we acquire largely through our relations with other people. A baby must "discover" that he is a separate entity, distinct from other things in his environment, before he can even begin to acquire attitudes toward himself. When a child does begin to develop a self-image, it occurs as a response to the reactions of others to his behavior. The sociologist, Charles Horton Cooley, referred to this process as the "looking-glass self": We see mirrored in the reactions of others an image of what we are.

Others' evaluations of a young child's behavior are translated more or less directly into self-evaluations. For the adult, self-esteem maintenance is a more complex process; but a self-image continues to be a social product. To be certain that we are what we think we are, we need periodic confirmation of this fact from others. The process of self-evaluation or self-esteem maintenance is therefore a social process, involving, at a minimum, one person who makes a claim that he warrants esteem and another person whose response indicates an acceptance or rejection of that claim.

A social "test" of self-esteem may be a very obvious one, as when we fish for a compliment, or a more subtle one, as when we act in ways we know others would approve even though they are not present to observe our actions. Likewise, the responses of others, which indicate whether we have passed or failed the test, may be as obvious as flattery or as subtle as a slight change in facial expression. Lasting social relationships are generally ones with others who are willing to see us in the same way we see ourselves. Each person's self-image, then, while existing as a set of attitudes, beliefs, and opinions held by the person about himself, is actually embedded in a set of social relationships that give it stability and continuity.

The fact that self-esteem maintenance is a social process and that not all the social roles we play are equally important for self-evaluation means that we need to find other people who are willing to evaluate us when we wish to be evaluated and to suspend judgment when we do not wish to be evaluated. In those roles in which we do evaluate ourselves and in terms of which we are attempting to maintain a favorable self-image, we need to find others whose definition of what constitutes an achievement is the same as ours. It is not always possible to meet both of these needs. The person whose sole concern in life is achievement at work and who spends all his time at the office may find that he is defined by others as a bad husband or father. The golfer who brags about breaking 90 may find the one who shoots in the 70s unimpressed.

The ability to anticipate or to predict whether others will evaluate us when we want them to and will use the same standards of judgment that we use in evaluating ourselves is seldom a problem with the people whom we know best. Even with people we do not know well, there are some cues that we can use to make such predictions. Every stable set of human interrelationships—whether it is a family, a friendship group, a formal organization, a community, or a total society—has an identifiable status structure. The term *status structure* refers to a hierarchy of persons based upon the extent to which they are accorded social honor. Differences in the amount of social honor accorded to persons may be produced by the unequal distribution of anything that is valued. In a work organization, status differences are based primarily upon the unequal distribution of skill, responsibility, and authority among the positions that make up the organization. An example of a less formalized status structure is in the typical high school class in which values like good grades, participation in school activities, athletic ability, and desirable personality attributes are among the criteria that determine whether one has high or low status.

The values that are used to assign status within any social organization, at either the small-group or the total societal level, reflect the major concerns of that social organization. The acquisition of status is a reward for achievement with regard to the major values within the organization, and the desire for status serves to motivate people to acquire whatever it is that is valued. To the extent that a stable and identifiable status structure exists within a social organization, it provides us with information regarding the values that are likely to be used by participants in that organization when they evaluate us.

If the criteria used for status assignment by others in the groups, formal organizations, community, and society in which we are a member are the same criteria that we use in evaluating ourselves, we would, in sociological terms, have a commitment to, or an identification with, these social organizations. The major values that shape our personalities (the criteria used in self-esteem maintenance) would be the same values that shape the organizations in which we are a member (the criteria used in status assignment). We would be motivated to achieve goals that are valued within these organizations because it is through the resulting status recognition from others that we confirm our own self-assessments. Alienation, as it is used in this chapter, means the opposite of commitment or identification as defined above. Alienation refers to a disjuncture between self-esteem maintenance and status-assignment systems. *We are alienated from others or from any organization in which we are a member to the extent that the criteria we use to evaluate ourselves are different from the criteria used by others in evaluating us.*

Some examples may help to clarify this use of the term alienation. A worker on an assembly line who has relatively low occupational status and sees little opportunity for advancement within the work organization may adjust to this situation by evaluating himself in exclusively non-work-related terms. To the extent that he is evaluated by others within the work organization in terms of his work role, however, he would be alienated from the organization. One probable consequence would be that he would not be motivated to contribute to the achievement of major organizational goals such as increasing output or decreasing costs. As a second example, most high school classes have some persons in them who are social isolates, who do not get good grades, and who appear to be unconcerned with any kind of achievement at school. It is possible that such persons are alienated from the school and from their classmates in the sense that what determines their level of self-esteem are hobbies, part-time work, or other non-school-related activities. As a third example, a Negro doctor who sees himself as a high achiever because of education, income, and occupational prestige may be alienated from a community which treats him with disrespect because of his race.

Each of these examples has involved a person who is regarded as having low status on some dimension that he does not use in evaluating himself. Generally speaking, the higher one is in a status hierarchy, the greater is the likelihood that he will use the values that account for his status when he evaluates himself. This follows from our assumption that support from others is required to confirm a favorable evaluation of self. Alienation is only one of a number of possible reactions to low status. Some people may react to an unfavorable evaluation from others with a mobility orientation; they may feel that their present low status is only a temporary condition and that they will eventually gain recognition for achievement. This is a stable or long-term response only if the person is successful in achieving some upward social mobility. As a second type of reaction, a person may feel that he is a failure if he is accorded low status. If the social role in which the person feels he is a failure is important to him in terms of maintaining his self-esteem, however, this is likely to be an untenable situation, and some sort of change in it will occur. The person will either lower his aspirations—a form of alienation if his aspirations become lower than the level others regard as an achievement—or try even harder to succeed, which would suggest a shift to a mobility orientation. Although alienation, or a withdrawal of concern with achievement, is not the only response to low status, it is a common one and is likely to be more stable than other responses. When what others think of us does not affect what we think of ourselves, we can accept low status with impunity.

The concept of alienation that has been developed above is similar to Seeman's definition of isolation but differs from it in several important respects. First, a person may be alienated from *any* social organization and not just from the total society. Second, the expression in Seeman's definition, "assigning a low reward value to goals or beliefs," has been elaborated so that the *reason* a low reward value is assigned is because the goals or beliefs have little relevance to self-assessment. Third, the expression, "goals or beliefs . . . typically highly valued [by others]," has been specified so that the values underlying the goals or beliefs are those used in the process of status assignment. With this definition of isolation from others, the meaning of self-estrangement and its relationship to isolation can be specified. People who *remain* in situations in which the criteria used in assigning status are different from the criteria they use in self-esteem maintenance (the alienated assembly-line worker or high school student) will minimize their expenditure of time or energy in the situation in order to conserve time and energy for what they regard as more important activities. The sense in which a person is alienated from his "self" under these circumstances is that his behavior in the situation has no direct relationship to what he thinks of himself. A person "invests" little of his self in situations in which he does not share criteria of evaluation with others because there would be little likelihood of a "payoff" on the investment.

In the sense in which we are using the term, alienation from others *necessarily* implies alienation from the self so long as we are involved in interaction with the other people from whom we are "isolated." If a person is not concerned with where he stands in the status structure of some social unit, he is isolated from it in the sense of assigning a "low reward value to goals or beliefs that are typically highly valued" in that social unit. Isolation necessarily implies self-estrangement, because it means that the person is not seeking recognition for what is regarded as an achievement by others within the social unit. We have assumed that in order to maintain an *evaluated* self-identity (*"bright* student," *"good* father," *"skillful* carpenter"), we need social support or confirmation from others that we are what we think we are. Lack of concern with status within a social unit is therefore evidence that we are not evaluating ourselves in terms of the self-identity relevant to that social unit. The student who does not care what his teachers or fellow students think of him is not evaluating himself within the school, the man who does not care whether his wife and children regard him as a good father is not evaluating himself within the family, and the carpenter who does not care whether his fellow workers regard him as skillful is not evaluating himself within the work group. During the time we participate in an activity that has no bearing upon our self-esteem we are self-estranged. Self-estrangement and isolation are simply opposite sides of the same coin and are the two major components of alienation as defined above.

## Industrialism and Alienation

The effect of industrialization upon the disjuncture between self-esteem maintenance and status-assignment processes is the major concern of this chapter. In Chapter 1 the village of San Miguel Milpas Altas in Guatemala was described as an example of a nonindustrial community. An examination of the ways in which the social structure of this community affects the relationship between how people evaluate themselves and how they are evaluated by others may help to clarify the connection between industrialism and alienation.

San Miguel Milpas Altas was characterized in Chapter 1 as a community in which there is very little social change, a relatively low level of structural differentiation, and a high level of social integration based upon mechanical solidarity. The status structure of a community having this set of attributes is likely to be a stable one in the sense that there is little shifting of people to higher or lower status levels, and the criteria that are used in status assignment remain relatively constant over time. A low level of structural differentiation means not only that everyone engages in essentially the same kinds of activities but also that there are few status levels and no extreme differences among the villagers in the amount of social honor they are accorded. The extent to which the San Migueleños share a common culture (that is, the extent to which they are socially integrated through mechanical solidarity) produces a community status structure in which there is a high level of consensus regarding the status placement of individuals and agreement regarding the criteria used in assigning status. Status criteria such as age and sex, which are unrelated to achievement in the usual sense of the word, are major determinants of the amount of respect a person receives in San Miguel Milpas Altas.[12]

With a status structure of this sort, alienation from the community is unlikely. First of all, the San Migueleño is rarely confronted with a social situation in the village that would lead him to question whether he really is what he thinks he is. Social situations that most often provoke this kind of questioning are ones involving people whose status is much higher than our own or people who evaluate us using unfamiliar status criteria. Neither of these conditions is characteristic of relationships among the villagers of San Miguel. Each person's image of himself is embedded in a stable set of social relationships through which it is constantly reinforced and reaffirmed. There is some question whether the self even develops as a distinct psychological entity under conditions in which a person's image of himself is never called into question.

The people of San Miguel, however, are regularly confronted by at least one alien set of values. Whenever they go into the city, the stable status distinctions of the village are no longer relevant and the San Migueleños are accorded the uniformly low status assigned to peasants by city dwellers. For most of the villagers, this status deprivation does not represent a serious threat to their image of themselves. Being defined as low-status peasants is regarded as an inconvenience if, for example, it means that they are the last to be waited on in stores, but does not appear to result in any lowering of self-esteem. Most of the people of San Miguel are alienated from the urban segment of Guatemalan society with its achievement-oriented value system in precisely the sense in which the term was defined above: Their image of themselves is anchored in the patterned social relations of the village, and the values that affect their self-esteem are different from the values used to assign status in Guatemala City.

There are some San Migueleños who appear to particularly resent being treated as peasants, and the way in which they differ from most other villagers is instructive. Although these people are not all at the top of the status structure in the village, they have been more successful economically than the others and are no longer merely subsistence-level farmers. One operates a small grain mill and charges other villagers a fee for grinding their corn. They are, in other words, achievers relative to other San Migueleños in terms of urban Guatemalan status criteria. Although they are unlikely ever to be recognized as achievers within this larger status structure, their advantage over other villagers is apparently a source of some self-esteem. Consequently, they are not alienated from the larger society, they are motivated to achieve in terms of its values, and they are resentful when their present level of achievement with respect to these values goes unrecognized.[13]

Aside from the complications introduced through contact with the outside world, there is apparently a high level of correspondence between the values used in self-esteem maintenance and those used in status assignment in this village. The social structural features of the village that contribute to this correspondence are the ones identified in Chapter 1 as the major factors differentiating nonindustrial from industrial societies.

Although social change, structural differentiation, and the decrease in the level of social integration were greatly accelerated by the Industrial Revolution, this pattern of change had begun to develop much earlier in the history of Western civilization. Industrialism was not superimposed upon a society having the attributes of San Miguel Milpas Altas but upon a much more complex social system.

The alienation of modern man had its roots in what Erich Fromm refers to as the process of *individuation* which accompanied the breakup of the medieval social structure. This social structure and, in fact, most of the patterned social arrangements throughout human history prior to the Middle Ages were similar in many important respects to the Guatemalan village discussed above. Peter Laslett describes this "world we have lost" as follows: "Time was, and it was all time up to 200 years ago, when the whole of life went forward in the family, in a circle of loved, familiar faces, known and fondled objects, all to human size. That time has gone forever. It makes us very different from our ancestors."[14]

One of the ways in which we are different, according to Fromm, is that we are free from the constraints of a small-group society and a fixed economic and political order. The member of a small-group society is never fully an individual in the sense of having independence of action but is only the sum of the stable set of roles that he enacts. Under these circumstances, self-image does not develop as an important component of personality and as a determinant of behavior because the answer to the question, "Who am I?" is so apparent that the question need not be asked. Fromm describes individuation, or the emergence of the individual in human history, as being similar in some ways to the developmental process in childhood and adolescence. The process of social maturation involves the severing of primary ties with parents and the development of freedom and independence of action. As the child matures he develops an image of self that serves as an internal guide to behavior substituting for the external constraints administered by his parents. Although the analogy is an imperfect one, Western man has, since the medieval period, achieved increasing freedom from small-group controls, or what has been described as the "tyranny of the genos," and has escaped from the fixed self-identity characteristic of a stable and rigid social order.

There was a price for this new-found freedom. There is a form of security in having a fixed identity in a stable social order that is rarely experienced today. When all one's social experience occurs within the framework of small-group controls, many of the problems afflicting modern man—insecurity, powerlessness, doubt, aloneness, or anxiety—are less likely to occur. In the following passage Fromm describes both the loss of security and the increase in freedom that accompany the process of individuation:

The breakdown of the medieval system of feudal society had one main significance for all classes of society: the individual was left alone and isolated. He was free. This freedom had a twofold result. Man was deprived of the security he had enjoyed, of the unquestionable feeling of belonging, and he was torn loose from the world which had satisfied his quest for security both economically and spiritually. He felt alone and anxious. But he was also free to act and to think independently, to become his own master and do with his life as he could—not as he was told to do.[15]

The significance of Fromm's analysis for our purpose is that alienation becomes a social problem only after the process of individuation has occurred. It was only after the individual's social experience began to encompass a much wider range than a small circle of family and friends that the disjuncture between self-esteem maintenance and status assignment became common. It is only in rapidly changing and highly differentiated societies that people are *frequently* exposed to sets of values at variance with their own. In *Escape from Freedom*, Fromm describes in detail how freedom and insecurity were products of changes occurring during the Renaissance and Reformation. Although the seeds of alienation were sown at that time, it is during the period since the Industrial Revolution that they have come to fruition.

Most of the expressions that have been used to describe the alienated industrial man can be seen as being related to the disjuncture between the status-assignment and self-esteem-maintenance processes. If industrial man is lonely, it is clearly not because he is physically isolated—urbanization has accompanied industrialization almost everywhere it has occurred. However, loneliness and anonymity can also be products of the generally shallow quality of interpersonal relationships in highly differentiated, industrial societies. Close or intimate social relations are always based upon a system of shared values in which each person is evaluated by others with the same criteria he uses in evaluating himself.

Apathy, indifference, a feeling of emptiness, or a lack of a sense of purpose in life all represent a second set of terms describing the experience of alienation. These experiences are products of a lack of identification with, or commitment to, *shared* goals and beliefs. In social psychological terms, the processes of identification and commitment involve self-evaluation in terms of the values on which social status is based. When we speak of a person being committed to a shared goal or identified with an organization within which the goal is shared, we mean that he is motivated to achieve the objectives of the organization. And it is through the achievement of organizational objectives that social status is acquired and self-assessments are confirmed.

A third way in which the consequences of alienation have been described is overconformity. Overconformity, along with loneliness and apathy, is a major issue in the social criticism of industrial society. And overconformity, along with loneliness and apathy, is produced, at least in part, by the disjuncture between self-esteem maintenance and status-assignment processes: Apathy and indifference discourage innovativeness, and ambiguities in complex urban-industrial status structures make conformity the path of least resistance.

The pervasiveness of alienation in industrial societies results from its relationship to characteristics inherent in the social structure of these societies. The major thesis in this chapter can be summarized as follows: Rapid social change, increased structural differentiation, decreased structural integration, and rationalization of social organization have produced widespread feelings of powerlessness, normlessness, or meaninglessness; this pattern of social experience reduces the correspondence between the criteria used in maintaining self-esteem and those used in assigning social status, which results in loneliness, apathy, or overconformity. Not everyone in industrial societies experiences alienation; and among those who do, some are more alienated than others. Difficulty in maintaining an adequate level of self-esteem is sufficiently widespread, however, to justify viewing alienation as an important problem of industrial society. In the next section of this chapter, we shall consider first the ways in which the structure of industrial society gives rise to feelings of powerlessness, normlessness, and meaninglessness and then the ways in which these feelings are related to alienation.

The complexity of industrial societies alone is sufficient to induce a sense of powerlessness. If power implies the ability to effectively control, even for the power elite there is objectively some degree of powerlessness. Only relative power is possible in an industrial society and not absolute power of the sort that could be wielded, for example, in a feudal society. The *experience* of power or of powerlessness is a matter of *relative* advantage or deprivation; and despite the difficulties of exercising effective control over complex social systems, there is an elite group in industrial societies, as in all societies, which can accurately be described as powerful.

What is unique to industrial societies is, first of all, the extent to which the *sense* of powerlessness pervades our experience and, second, the impersonality of the forces which produce it. We have noted that preindustrial societies are characterized by a high level of group control of behavior. These constraints are unlikely to be perceived as being external to the individual or imposed upon him. Where norms and values are widely shared and enforced through informal social processes, the individual member of the group is less likely to *feel* powerless, although objectively speaking, he may be so. With the process of individuation and the imposition of external controls such as laws or bureaucratic regulations by a power elite, having power or not having power may be seen as genuine alternatives. It is under these circumstances that powerlessness is apt to be *experienced* as a form of deprivation. The amount of rationalization required by the complexity of industrial societies means that there are few areas of our experience that are unaffected either directly or indirectly by some form of external regulation.

The impersonality of these constraints in industrial societies contributes in an important way to the sense of powerlessness. If the only source of oppressive control is a totalitarian leader, he can be overthrown. If the source is an entire way of life, revolution is a less effective response. The idea that "you can't beat the system" expresses the impotence of people confronted by a rationalized and impersonal system of social control. Even where the controls are administered personally, as in a foreman-worker relationship, the basis of the control is recognized as being within the system rather than the person. When a foreman gives an unpopular order, it is generally understood that he is simply doing his job. A common response to the sense of powerlessness resulting from pervasive impersonal controls is apathy. And apathy, as we shall see presently, is a symptom of alienation as defined above.

One reflection of the difficulty in dealing with the complex control structure of industrial societies is the creation of the *ombudsman* role. *Ombudsman* is a Swedish word meaning, literally, "one who represents someone." The position was developed in Scandinavian countries to serve as an appeal mechanism circumventing the usual channels through which the complaints of private citizens are heard. The system has spread to other countries, and in fact, an *ombudsman* was recently appointed at Michigan State University with the responsibility to "assist students in accomplishing the expeditious settlement of their problems." The *ombudsman's* function reflects not only the complexity of control systems but also the unequal distribution of ability to cope with these systems: The *ombudsman's* clientele are private citizens who are most likely to experience powerlessness when faced with the structural and procedural complexity of bureaucratic organizations. Ability to deal with and "beat" the system is most directly in proportion to experience in large, formal organizations, particularly at higher administrative levels, and to the amount of formal education. For this reason, a sense of powerlessness and resulting apathy are more common among people in lower- than in higher-status occupations. People likely to experience powerlessness, however, represent a substantial majority of the population in industrial societies.

With the breakup of the medieval social order, men achieved freedom from personalized small-group controls. The deterioration of *any* established social order is followed by a period in which social controls are at a minimum. The experience of new African nations as they develop from tribal societies today is a case in point. An industrial society, however, requires a high level of social control in order to achieve sufficient integration of its complex interdependent structure. Impersonal, rationalized controls are the only possible means to achieve this integration. In mature industrial societies there is much less of the kind of freedom that Fromm described as having developed with the Renaissance. For a substantial segment of the population today, there is very little control over the important events that shape their lives.

Normlessness, or the feeling that it is impossible to achieve generally accepted goals through socially approved means, is also a product of the social structure of industrial societies. But it is not a universal experience in these societies and, like powerlessness, is more common in the working and lower classes than in the middle or upper. Opportunity for upward social mobility is, in fact, greater in industrial than in preindustrial societies. However, there has never been genuine equality of opportunity in the sense that ability alone was the determinant of success. In mature industrial societies, advancement most often takes the form of movement through a series of progressively more prestigeful positions in a bureaucratic organization. The bottom rung of this mobility ladder has moved steadily upward as the amount of skill and knowledge required in an increasingly complex occupational system has grown. In order to see advancement as a realistic possibility, it has become necessary to enter the labor force at a higher level than was the case in the last century; and this usually means entering with much more formal education. Even the bottom step on the mobility ladder today is reserved for the most part for the high school or, increasingly, the college graduate. This does not necessarily mean that the overall rate of upward social mobility has declined. There are many more people with a college degree today than in the past. It does mean that the goal of economic achievement is not likely to be attained by those who are unable to get the requisite amount of education. Some evidence of the extent to which a differentiated and rationalized economic system places a premium upon formal education was presented in Chapter 2.

There have been people without much hope for advancement at the bottom of the class structure in all societies. It is particularly in industrial societies that there is a strong onus upon the failure to achieve. The historical process of individuation, along with a relatively open class system, placed the burden of success or failure upon the individual. Because economic development has so monopolized the attention and energy of industrial man, economic achievement has become the major determinant of social status. The whole culture of industrialism is built around the goal of continued economic growth, and a man's work is consequently the most common measure of his worth. In addition to the ways in which the present structure of industrial society emphasizes individual economic achievement, there is an element of the preindustrial cultural heritage of Western civilization that also has this effect. One part of what has been called the Protestant ethic was the idea that success in one's calling was an "outward sign of inner grace," or an indication of being among the saved rather than the damned.[16] Equating wealth with virtue and poverty with sin was an easy transition from this Calvinist doctrine. The contemporary secular version of this idea is the predominantly middle-class notion that the basis for both social status and self-esteem *should* be occupational success.

Although there is more or less continuous and universal exposure to the idea that there is virtue in affluence, it is clear that there is a substantial segment of the population in all industrial societies which cannot reasonably aspire to this goal. While the goal is universally prescribed, the means are not universally available. Criminologists have suggested that many types of crime can be explained by norm-lessness of this type. However, a much more common response among people who have little hope of becoming high achievers economically is to denigrate the importance of economic achievement. In contrast to the earlier stages of industrialization in which virtue and hard work were assumed to be the bases for success, luck or fate are more often used to explain success or failure today. Aphorisms such as "early to bed and early to rise make a man healthy, wealthy, and wise" have been replaced by more cynical views such as "it is not what you know but who you know." This change is reflected in literature in the difference between what accounted for the success of Horatio Alger and what accounts for the success of the hero in contemporary novels such as *Room at the Top*. Andrew Carnegie, Jay Gould, and Henry Ford were among the folk heroes of an earlier era; today it is not the heroic producer but the heroic consumer—the big spender—who is likely to be a well-known public figure. These cynical views are particularly common among people in working- and lower-class positions; and to the extent that this indicates a rejection of the value placed upon economic success, they are alienated from the majority of the society for whom this value is important. We shall return to this issue again in a later section of this chapter.

Although normlessness is related to the lack of integration between ends and means and to the rationalization of mobility channels in industrial societies, *meaninglessness* in these societies is particularly a product of rapid change and structural differentiation. The fractionated character of industrial life means that each individual plays many more social roles and, consequently, has many more self-identities than was the case in the past. Many of the most common social relations of industrial man, such as the relationship between clerk and customer or employer and employee, involve only a narrow range of the ideas about himself that constitute his self-image. His relations with his family, his friends, and with the people with whom he works are isolated from each other and often involve distinctly different conceptions of self and distinctly different bases for maintaining self-esteem. Although individual social encounters may be meaningful in the sense that their outcome can be predicted—the customer can anticipate the behavior of the clerk—the overall pattern of life is less meaningful. Rapid social change and the segmented character of social experience make it difficult to see any clear trajectory for one's life.

The concept of meaninglessness has most often been applied to the effect of extensive division of labor upon the job of the industrial worker. The narrowly specialized tasks in most factories mean that individual workers have little sense of, or concern for, how their jobs relate to the total production process. This use of meaninglessness is somewhat different from Seeman's definition of the term but is clearly related to it. The worker whose responsibilities are limited to a minute portion of the operations within a production organization is less able to predict the outcome of his or others' behavior in any other than his immediate task area. The rationalization process makes the outcome of particular situations predictable and hence meaningful, but structural differentiation restricts this meaning to only bits and pieces of social experience. For many people in the labor force of industrial societies, work has no meaningful relationship to the rest of life except the purely instrumental one of providing income. The contrast between this aspect of industrial societies and the integration of work with other areas of experience on the family farm or business that was characteristic of the preindustrial period is a particularly striking one.

There has been a general decline in industrial societies in the extent to which people are able to see the interrelations among events and to act intelligently on the basis of this insight. Karl Mannheim refers to this process as a decline in "substantial rationality."[17] In the performance of highly specialized tasks, activities become routinized and it becomes much easier simply to conform to the external controls regulating behavior than to reason why, how, or when things should be done. Mannheim argues that as the rationalization of society has increased, the capacity of people to think independently and arrive at their own judgments about things has decreased. It is not only the process of rationalization that is involved but also the complexity and segmentation of industrial society that produce isolated social roles and self-identities, thereby increasing the difficulty in seeing meaningful interrelationships among events. As the *possibility* for relating specific areas of experience to any overall life pattern declines, the *motivation* to do so may also decline, at which point "substantial irrationality" becomes likely. Areas of experience may be meaningful either intrinsically or because of their relationship to a more general life pattern or trajectory. Where there is neither the possibility nor the desire to relate an activity to broader areas of experience and where the activity is not meaningful in itself, routinization and overconformity are likely to result. For the worker whose job is both too narrowly specialized to be intrinsically meaningful and isolated physically and socially from the rest of his experience, work is likely to be reduced to a routine for which little "substantial rationality" is required.

In the discussion of meaninglessness we have so far considered two related but somewhat distinct senses in which the term can be used. One is associated primarily with structural differentiation and involves the inability to find meaning in an activity because it is unrelated to any larger pattern of life experience. The other is most directly a consequence of rapid social change and involves the inability to accurately predict the outcome of social situations. Both types of meaninglessness may result in overconformity. It was noted above that an activity which has no relationship to broader and more important areas of our lives is likely to become routinized, and conformity to whatever regulations exist becomes the "path of least resistance." Deviation is regarded as not worth the trouble it causes, and there is little incentive to be innovative. The behavior of semi-skilled production and clerical workers generally fits this pattern.

Meaninglessness of the second type—the inability to accurately predict behavioral outcomes or uncertainty regarding what one should do—may produce another motive for conformity: The easiest course of action when one is uncertain of what is appropriate is simply to do what others are doing. This pattern of behavior has been called *other-direction* by David Riesman.[18] Riesman describes a series of character types beginning, historically, with *tradition-directed*, which characterizes a person whose behavior is guided by a stable set of traditions of the sort that existed in small-group societies during the agricultural-craft preindustrial period. The next character type he terms the *inner-directed*. The inner-directed person is guided by a set of values that he regards as *his own*. The perception of values as one's *own* values develops with the process of individuation and is unlikely to occur in traditional societies where there are few value differences. The idea of a personal value system implies a contrasting set of values held by someone else. The increasing structural differentiation of industrial society in the early stages of industrialization is likely to produce such value conflicts, and the inner-directed character type is most characteristic of this period. As the pace of social change accelerates and the degree of structural differentiation increases in the later stages of this period, the individual can no longer be so certain that his own values are correct or appropriate. He is exposed to a wider range of alternative values among the people with whom he comes in contact and may perceive that values he acquired in the past are no longer appropriate to changed conditions in the present. These circumstances introduce an increasing element of uncertainty (or meaninglessness) into social encounters. The other-directed character type responds to this uncertainty by "doing unto others what he sees others doing unto him." Other-direction is particularly common in mature industrial societies but may occur as a response to meaninglessness at any stage of development.

The middle-class bureaucrat is apparently especially susceptible to other-directedness. The "organization man," the "man in the grey flannel suit," and the "status seekers" are expressions that have been used to describe other-directed types who are, for the most part, moderately successful employees of large organizations. The emphasis here is particularly upon meaninglessness and ambiguity of status structures. What is required to advance or to gain prestige or honor in contemporary complex organizations is often unclear. Selection for promotion is based in part upon the possession of personality attributes that are valued by one's superior but which are never clearly spelled out as conditions for promotion. What constitutes skill in job performance is clear and measurable only in occupations such as the skilled trades and in most professions where there is some easily identifiable end product of individual effort. Where success or failure at work is measured in terms of the efficiency of a department, the profitability of an enterprise, or public acceptance of a product or service, achievement is an organizational rather than an individual process. When recognition of individual achievement occurs, the social honor it involves may not extend beyond the organization—the newly promoted department manager may be treated with no more deference by most people outside the organization than when he was an assistant manager.

The combination of ill-defined status criteria, promotion based upon unspecified personality attributes, and the lack of carry-over of work-related achievements into non-work-related social encounters leads many people into an other-directed quest for symbols of status. Under conditions of rapid social change and extensive structural differentiation, the security that comes from general recognition of achievement requires the acquisition of generally accepted symbols of achievement. The self-identities involved in maintaining self-esteem may be more closely related to status *symbols* than to the *achievements* they presumably symbolize. For example, the self-identity owner-of-the-biggest-and-fastest-powerboat-on-the-lake may be more important for self-esteem than the self-identity most-efficient-deputy-assistant-director-in-the-bureau. This preoccupation with status symbols leads to what have been called status cycles in which concern with social status (or, in other words, with confirming an evaluated image of self) occurs only through the display of symbols of affluence on weekends and vacations. Through careful budgeting, periodic display of affluence may be possible for the file clerk as well as the company president. Where status symbols are not closely tied to particular levels of achievement, they become capricious and subject to fads and fashions. Concern with what is currently "in" or with how to become a member of the "in-crowd" reflects the other-directed conformity produced by ambiguities in the status-assignment process.

We have now examined the meaning and some of the consequences of powerlessness, normlessness, and meaninglessness in mature industrial societies. Apathy has been described as one consequence of powerlessness, lowering of aspirations as a consequence of normlessness, and overconformity as a consequence of meaninglessness. These three conditions are common problems in industrial societies; they are products of inherent social structural features of such societies; and they represent the *alienated* responses to powerlessness, normlessness, and meaninglessness. They are not, however, the only possible responses to these conditions.

The person who responds to lack of power, for example, by *seeking to achieve it* is not alienated. The attempt to gain power in an organization, community, or society reflects commitment to, rather than isolation from, these social units and is evidence that self-esteem is affected by one's standing in the status structure of the unit. Apathy, on the other hand, means that there is little or no investment of self. A person cannot be apathetic about an activity that has an important bearing upon what he thinks of himself. Passive acceptance of an inability to influence the conditions of participation within any social unit implies a lack of concern with the major values that structure the unit and, therefore, represents alienation from it.

The connection between apathy and alienation is easiest to see where the relationship between the individual and the social unit is a relatively simple one. The employee who has invested little of his self in the work role and who is, consequently, not seeking a return on such an investment in the form of recognition for achievement can afford to be apathetic regarding his inability to control the events that affect his status at work. In a complex relationship such as that between the individual and the society of which he is a member, both apathy and alienation are likely to be limited to some segment of this relationship. For example, political apathy in the form of failure to vote in elections does not necessarily reflect alienation from American society. It does suggest that the individual is not evaluating himself in terms of the identity "good citizen" and that he is alienated from that segment of the society which regards this as an important social role.

Similarly, lowering of aspirations is only one of several possible responses to the perception that the only way to achieve generally valued goals is through socially unapproved means. Among other reactions to normlessness are the alternative responses to low status that were mentioned above: a mobility orientation and a lowering of self-esteem. A third possibility is to use illegitimate means to achieve the goal. All three of these responses represent commitment to, rather than alienation from the social unit within which the goal is valued. The mobility, or "if at first you don't succeed, try, try again," orientation suggests that attainment of the goal is important for maintaining self-esteem and that recognition from others for attaining it will be necessary in order to do so. The use of socially unapproved means also suggests an investment of self in the quest for the goal, as does a lowering of self-esteem if it is not attained. Lowering one's aspirations or denying the desirability of the goal, however, represents alienation from others who continue to value the goal; it means that the individual is being evaluated by others in ways in which he no longer evaluates himself. The student who is unable to get good grades and who, rather than feeling that he is a failure, trying harder, or cheating, decides that getting good grades is really not as important as being popular on the campus has selected the alienated response to normlessness.

Conformity as a response to meaninglessness is also an example of alienation. The lack of "substantial rationality," the suspension of individual judgment, and the conformity that characterize the on-the-job behavior of semiskilled production and clerical workers can be accounted for by the fact that work is less important than other activities as a basis for maintaining self-esteem. Conformity, as the course of least resistance, becomes the most reasonable course in an activity that is not defined as important.

The alienation of the other-directed status seeker is of a slightly different order. We noted above that the major symbols of status in industrial society have become detached from specific levels and types of achievement. The process of maintaining self-esteem to the extent that it involves exclusively the acquisition of these status symbols is therefore also detached from specific levels or types of achievement. If self-esteem is invested primarily in expensive automobiles, vacations in exotic places, powerful outboard motors, and large picture windows (though the view may be limited to the neighbor's picture window), other activities including work become simply instrumental—a means to more successful manipulation of status symbols. The conformity or other-directedness of the organization man at work may reflect not only uncertainty regarding the bases for advancement but also the conviction that the major payoff in status recognition may occur in his role as consumer rather than producer. Uncertainties regarding the possibility of maintaining an adequate level of self-esteem through activities within the work organization may *produce* alienation from the work organization and a primary commitment to maintaining self-esteem through leisure activities. The people most susceptible to this pattern of alienation are apparently middle-level managers in large organizations whose incomes are high enough to permit successful manipulation of status symbols and whose chances for promotion to upper-level managerial positions are sufficiently remote to encourage self-esteem testing outside the work role.

The vagaries of the quest for status symbols—a status seeker may furnish his house with pop art only to discover that op art is now "in"—pose other problems for maintaining self-esteem. If avoiding alienation requires a correspondence between the criteria used in evaluation of self and the criteria used in evaluation by others, instability or rapid change in what is valued by others requires a constant process of adjustment of self-image. It is only those who are other-directed who can remain consistently integrated into the "in-group" and sufficiently alienated from the "out-group."

Overconformity and other types of alienation have been treated by Fromm, among others, as *general* aspects of the experience of industrial man. The conditions producing alienation—powerlessness, normlessness, and meaninglessness—may be perceived as all-encompassing if a person feels unable to control any of the major factors influencing his life, unable to achieve any important goals through legitimate means, or unable to find any meaning in life. The consequence may be a nonpurposive or non-goal-directed life-style in which people simply drift through day-to-day activities without seeing any broader pattern in their lives. The absence of a firm anchorage for self-concept in social units whose goals are relevant for both social status and self-esteem is a major factor producing this experience. And apathy, low aspirations, and overconformity are common elements of the nonpurposive life-style.

Although there are undoubtedly many people in industrial societies who experience this form of alienation, it is clearly not a universal affliction. Powerlessness, normlessness, and meaninglessness are not distributed evenly throughout the population; and alienation is only one among several possible responses to these conditions. A general alienation from industrialism as a way of life is most often found among the economically disadvantaged. In a society whose major institutions are structured primarily around the goal of continuous economic growth, the economic underachiever is particularly susceptible to alienation. The concluding section of this chapter will deal with the relationship between poverty and alienation.

We are concerned in this book not only with the alienated orientation toward life, but also with alienation as a response to specific social roles. Being alienated in one or more social roles while being committed to others is an almost universal experience in highly differentiated societies. For alienation to represent a social problem under these circumstances, it would have to be a common occurrence in such important and status-producing social roles as the occupational role, familial role, or citizen role.

Alienation in the occupational role would appear to qualify as a social problem in terms both of its frequency and of the seriousness of its consequences. There are many occupations in industrial societies that are likely to induce a sense of powerlessness, normlessness, or meaninglessness in the work setting. These conditions often result in behavior on the job reflecting apathy, low aspirations, over-conformity, or other symptoms of alienation from work. Among the factors that determine whether alienation will result from power-lessness, normlessness, and meaninglessness are the status level of the occupation, opportunity for upward mobility, variation in the occupational status level of work associates, length of training time for the occupation, and the extent of integration of the work role with other areas of social experience. The next section of this chapter will focus specifically upon alienation in the occupational role.

### Alienation from Work

Everyone engages in some activities that have little bearing upon what he thinks of himself and in which he is relatively unconcerned about evaluations by others. The occasional bowler or bridge player for whom winning is of no particular consequence are cases in point. For the most part, we tend to minimize our participation in activities from which we are alienated. There are some activities, however, in which participation is on a less voluntary basis, and work is one of these.[19] Because so much of the time of such a large proportion of the population is spent in some form of gainful employment, an occupational structure that produces alienation from work has important consequences for the quality of existence in industrial society.

A substantial proportion, if not a majority, of the labor force in industrial societies are in jobs that would appear likely to produce alienation from work.

Everett Hughes has described a man's work as "one of the things by which he is judged, and certainly one of the significant things by which he judges himself."[20] Although this is undoubtedly often the case, it is by no means clear that it is universally so. In occupationally homogeneous, nonindustrial communities such as San Miguel Milpas Altas, work is not a particularly adequate basis for either status differentiation or self-evaluation.[21] A status hierarchy develops only where there is *unequal* distribution of something that is valued, and self-esteem can be maintained only with the social support represented by recognition for achievement—a process that implies the existence of a status hierarchy. Even where there are clear status differences among occupations, as in industrial societies, it does not necessarily follow that everyone evaluates himself in terms of his work. Because of the multidimensional character of social status in societies like our own, there is the possibility of selection among a variety of criteria for judging others as well as one's self. The prestigiousness of one's occupation and the quality of work-role performance are only two among many status criteria.

The idea that occupational achievement *should* have an important bearing upon what a person thinks of himself is very common among middle-class Americans. For this reason, it is sometimes difficult for people with a middle-class background to believe that anyone could be unsuccessful at work and not feel that he was a failure. The industrial worker who does not aspire to higher-status jobs is frequently regarded as an unambitious or untalented *person*. This view rests upon the assumption that ambition and talent are *necessarily* expressed through work and fails to recognize that non-work-related achievements may be an important basis for social status. The person who is "lazy" at work may be acclaimed by his friends, relatives, and neighbors for the ambitious home-improvement projects he undertakes.

There has been very little research by sociologists or social psychologists bearing directly upon the question of what differentiates people who evaluate themselves in terms of work from those who do not. If we assume, however, that any activity that affects self-esteem is likely to be perceived as an *important* activity, there is a considerable amount of research evidence from which we can infer differences in alienation from work. Many studies have demonstrated that more people in high-status occupations than in low-status occupations regard work as an important activity. Morse and Weiss, in a study of a national sample of employed males, found that a sense of accomplishment on the job, interest in a particular task area, and in general, the assigning of importance to a specific work role were more characteristic of professional and managerial than of clerical and blue-collar workers.[22] Chinoy reports that success in life to automobile workers means the achievement of primarily non-work-related goals.[23] Hyman cites evidence that there is less working-class than middle- or upper-class concern with occupational success.[24] Mills suggests that for the "white-collar masses," as for wage workers generally, the job is not intrinsically meaningful and success, in the sense of technical craftsmanship, is not regarded as an end in itself.[25] Riesman and Bloomberg suggest that members of the working-class whose jobs are not distinguishable in terms of a clearly specified prestige hierarchy seek leisure activities in which status comparisons are possible.[26] Blum, in a study of packinghouse workers, notes the quest for self-expression in leisure activities, relates this to the absence of meaningful qualitative distinctions in work-role performance, and reports that most packinghouse workers have "lowered their level of aspiration to the emptiness of the job and as a result direct their energies toward money and activities outside the factory."[27] Dubin found that work and the work place were not "central life interests" for almost three-fourths of a sample of industrial workers whom he studied;[28] and Orzack, using the same set of questions as Dubin, found that for four out of five of the registered nurses he studied, work and the work place were "central life interests."[29] The results of a study by Lyman indicate that blue-collar workers most often see work as a means to provide income, and white-collar workers value intrinsic aspects of the job and the opportunities it provides for self-expression.[30] Wilensky, in a study of 1,156 employed men in Detroit, found that more than three times as many of those from a low socioeconomic level as from a high socioeconomic level were "indifferent" to work. Indifference in this study meant specifically that work was unrelated to major attributes of self-image.[31]

Other studies with similar findings might be cited. The general pattern that emerges from these studies in that success at work is not so important to people in lower-status occupations. These research findings are what we would expect if we interpret them in terms of the conception of alienation developed above. When we say an occupation has low status, we mean that relatively few people would be willing to act toward persons in that occupation in ways that would support a favorable self-image based upon success at work. One response to the inability to confirm a favorable self-image at work is to evaluate one's self exclusively with non-work-related values. It is possible that a person may evaluate himself in terms of how good he is at what he does rather than of how his occupation ranks in comparison with other occupations. The distinction involved here is between an *intra*positional evaluation ("Jones is a better doctor than Smith") and an *inter*positional evaluation ("it is better to be a doctor than a farm laborer"). The lower the general status of an occupation, the fewer are the people who assign value to the criteria that distinguish good performance on the job from poor performance on the job. A farm laborer may be famous among other farm laborers for his strength, and a structural-steel worker may be famous among other structural-steel workers for his courage. Neither strength nor courage, however, is *generally* accepted as an important occupational value, whereas skill, knowledge, and initiative—which are used to distinguish good doctors from bad doctors or good lawyers from bad lawyers—are almost universally regarded as important occupational values. In many narrowly specialized, lower-status occupations it is difficult to find *any* generally accepted basis for differentiating good from bad work performance. The assembly-line worker in the factory and the lower-level clerical worker in the office do not customarily see themselves nor are they customarily seen by others as being good or bad at what they do for a living.

The general proposition that is suggested here is that the smaller the number of people willing to accord high status for achievement at work, the more difficult it is to confirm a favorable image of self based upon this achievement and the greater is the likelihood of being alienated from work. In lower-status occupations, whether the basis for self-evaluation is intrapositional or interpositional, the probability of social support for self-esteem based upon work is smaller, and the probability of self-evaluation in *non*-work-related terms is therefore greater. Two exceptions to this proposition should be noted.

First, a person in a low-status occupation may see himself as being in this position only temporarily. He may, in other words, be mobility-oriented instead of being alienated. A management trainee who has been placed temporarily in an assembly-line job in order to become familiar with plant operations is not at all likely either to feel that he is a failure or to become alienated from work as a result. He can see a well-defined sequence of jobs through which he can move to more prestigious positions. An apprentice in a skilled trade may have a similar view of his prospects. A mobility orientation is likely to be characteristic of *most* new entrants into the labor force. Almost all young people in industrial societies are exposed in some measure to the value placed upon occupational success, and they are likely to begin their careers with this goal in mind. If, however, entry into the labor force is through a low-status occupation that is not part of a training program and if the entrant lacks the education, skills, or social graces necessary for advancement, he may very soon learn that his chances for upward social mobility are limited. Eli Chinoy has described a "chronology of aspirations" among automobile workers in which there is a steady decline in occupational-aspiration levels during the early years of work experience.[32]

The initial reaction of the person who sees what he once regarded as a temporary low-status job becoming a permanent one is likely to be a generalized sense of personal failure. A common rationalization, in the psychological sense of the term, for failure at work is to suggest to oneself and others that success at work is not important. If the person finds social support for this view and begins to find non-work-related ways in which to build a favorable self-image, the rationalization becomes the reality. He is genuinely no longer concerned with success at work because he no longer has any of his self-esteem invested in this area of his life. At this point his experience of work involves alienation both from self and from others who regard work as a basis for status assignment. Although we have used the unsuccessful new entrant into the labor force to illustrate the sequence of developments from a mobility orientation to alienation from work, the middle-aged organization man who, after some initial success, finds further mobility blocked might have been an equally appropriate illustration of the process.

There is a second exception to the generalization that people in lower-status occupations tend to be alienated from work. The first alternative to alienation described above—a mobility orientation— involves a recognition that one is, at least temporarily, in a low-status position and implies an acceptance of the value system in terms of which the occupation is assigned a low-status rating. The desire to move to a higher-status occupation is the evidence that this is so. The characteristic response of persons in some lower-status occupations, however, is pride in their work and a rejection of the value system generally used to allocate status among occupations. The orientation toward work of the jazz musician illustrates this pattern. Being a jazz musician is not regarded by most people as an accomplishment, and few people know enough about music to distinguish between a good and a bad performance. Professional jazz musicians, however, appear to be highly committed to their occupation in the sense of evaluating themselves in terms of success in the work role. The response to this discrepancy between how they evaluate themselves and how they are evaluated by others is to isolate themselves from the public as much as possible. Distinctive patterns of dress and speech serve to differentiate musicians—who can be counted upon to use the "right" standards for assigning occupational status— from "squares" who use the "wrong" standards. The pattern of working hours, the absence of a fixed place of employment, and the fact that interaction on the job can be limited to other musicians also contribute to this isolation. Jazz musicians constitute a distinct occupational community with a unique set of criteria for evaluating occupational success. Status arrangements within this occupational community encompass a broad span of status distinctions ranging down from an internationally recognized elite.

Although the jazz musician is a particularly good example of this pattern, there are other occupations in which it may be found. Some other examples of socially and physically isolated workers who appear to have a greater commitment to work than would be expected on a basis of the status level of their occupation are structural-steel workers, combat infantrymen, merchant seamen, and longshoremen. The general proposition that is suggested by these examples is that commitment to work rather than alienation from work may be possible in lower-status occupations where there is a clear intrapositional status hierarchy and isolation from others who assign occupational status on a basis of different criteria.

In summarizing the factors that produce alienation from work, low occupational status would appear to be most critical because it is directly related to difficulty in finding social support for a favorable work identity. Low-status occupations also involve, for the most part, narrowly defined tasks in which it is hard to distinguish skillful from unskillful performance of the job. There is usually no easily identified end product of individual effort that can be compared with that of others as a test of self-esteem. In addition, most low-status occupations are dead-end jobs in the sense that there are limited opportunities for advancement into more prestigious positions. Mobility aspirations become increasingly unrealistic at progressively lower levels of the occupational-status hierarchy.

A final attribute of low-status occupations that encourages alienation from work is that people in these jobs less often come into contact with others at work who have either higher or lower status than their own. The doctor, the lawyer, the plumber, and the salesman, in the course of their work, regularly interact with people at different occupational-status levels. The on-the-job social relationships of semiskilled machine operators and clerical workers, however, are largely limited to people in these same occupations. Regular contact with people at *lower* status levels provides support for a favorable self-image based upon work. The small businessman in a lower-class neighborhood is frequently reminded that he is a relatively high

achiever. Regular contact at work with people at a *higher* occupational-status level makes it difficult to avoid evaluation of self in terms
of the work role and encourages mobility aspirations. Willie Loman,
the central character in Arthur Miller's *Death of a Salesman*, is an
example of a person with an extreme commitment to occupational
success buttressed by past contacts with prestigeful clients. The social
relationships of a person whose work associates are all at his own
status level, however, neither enhance nor threaten his work identity and consequently make it easier to retain an *unevaluated* image
of self in the work role. The assembly-line worker who has little to
gain by evaluating himself in terms of either his job or the quality
of his performance of it is rarely forced to do so because his work
seldom brings him into contact with people whose jobs or levels of
work-role performance are different from his own. It was argued
above that isolation from people in other occupations, as in the case
of the jazz musician, could facilitate commitment to work. The
difference between this pattern and that of the assembly-line worker
lies in the possibility for *intra*positional status distinctions. The jazz
musician frequently works with people who are generally regarded
as better or worse musicians than he is.

The pattern of relatively low interpositional status, meaningless
intrapositional-status distinctions, limited possibility for upward mobility, and restriction of work associates to persons at the same status
level is most characteristic of unskilled laborers, semiskilled machine
operators, and lower-level clerical workers. These occupational categories constituted 39.4 percent of the American labor force in 1965.
Of course, not all the persons in these occupations are alienated from
work. Young people are, in particular, more likely to have a mobility
orientation than to be alienated. The studies referred to above, however, suggest that a substantial proportion of the people in these jobs
see their work as an instrumental activity, evaluate themselves in
terms of non-work-related activities, and are therefore alienated from
work in the sense in which we are using the term in this chapter.
If we add some service workers, some older lower-level managers and
officials with limited opportunity for promotion, and some lower-
status sales workers—all of whose circumstances approximate the

conditions encouraging alienation—it seems likely that at least half of the American labor force is alienated from work. And this may be a conservative estimate. Harold Wilensky, in the study previously cited, concludes that "on balance, the vast majority of Americans are 'playing it cool,' neither strongly wedded to the job nor feeling it to be an intense threat to their identity. . . . the general impression from these and other data is that the typical American man is lightly committed to his work."[33]

There is potentially a wide variety of behavioral consequences of this failure to evaluate the self-identity associated with the work role. Research by industrial sociologists and psychologists indicates that apathy, low aspirations, and overconformity—identified above as common behavioral indicators of alienation—are frequent responses to unskilled and semiskilled jobs. There are some occupations, however, in which behavior and attitudes suggesting alienation are seldom found. The occupational category in which there is *least* likely to be alienation from work is the professions. Technological change has tended to increase rather than decrease the amount of skill and responsibility involved in these occupations. The professional typically has considerable freedom at work and is unlikely to see himself as powerless. His job is generally meaningful to him because there is an important and clearly identifiable end product of his efforts. Normlessness is not a problem since increasing recognition for professional competence provides him with a legitimate means of achieving higher social status. The nature of his work characteristically brings the professional into contact with people in a broad range of occupational-status levels, most of which are lower than his own. This combination of circumstances increases the likelihood that the professional will evaluate himself in terms of his work and will be successful in finding social support for a favorable work identity. If the professional does not appear to be actively seeking status recognition, it may be that his level of achievement is sufficiently high that he needs only to maintain rather than enhance his status level in order to support a favorable self-identity in the work role. Research dealing with the attitudes of professionals indicates that they do, in fact, have a high level of commitment to work.

The skilled trades possess many of these same attributes and represent a second occupational category in which alienation from work is unlikely. Although the status level of the skilled trades falls in the middle range when compared with all other occupations, skilled workers are an elite group among manual workers. The process of mechanization has eliminated many craft occupations but has tended to increase the skill level required in those that remain; it has also created some new highly skilled trades. With the possible exception of some of the skilled workers who are employed by large organizations, neither powerlessness, meaninglessness, nor normlessness is likely to be experienced by people in these occupations. Again, the studies that have been done support the expectation, based upon these conditions, that skilled tradesmen are committed to, rather than alienated from, work.

Both the traditional professions and the skilled trades antedated the period of mechanization in industrial societies; it is in the semi-skilled blue-collar and white-collar occupations created by the mechanization process that alienation from work is most likely. The other major preindustrial occupation, farming, is also characterized by a relatively high level of commitment to work. Farming shares some of the characteristics of the professions and skilled trades, including freedom from close supervision and an identifiable end product of individual effort that can be meaningfully compared with that of others. Farmers are not accorded high social status by urban standards but are, for the most part, socially isolated from the people who hold these standards. There is another job attribute that farming has in common with the professions and, to a lesser degree, with the skilled trades that tends to prevent alienation from work. For the farmer and the professional, work is not isolated or differentiated from the rest of their social experience but is highly integrated with it. Semi-skilled factory and office workers seldom even see the people they work with away from the factory or office, but the professional's closest friends are most likely to be chosen from among his colleagues. The farmer's "colleagues" are most often members of his family. The work role of the farmer and of the professional does not

have a separate and instrumental function but is an integral part of their total life experience. The consequence of this is that there is not a work identity that is clearly distinguishable and isolated from an image of self in other social contexts. If the "image of self at work" cannot be easily distinguished from the "image of self in the family," the "image of self in relations with close friends," or any other important social relationship, the process of maintaining a favorable self-image necessarily requires some success in the work role.[34] This does not mean that all professionals, skilled tradesmen, and farmers are necessarily committed to their work. It is possible, although more difficult, for the person who is a failure in one of these occupations to isolate himself from his colleagues and others who would regard him as a failure and, as a result, to sustain a view of work as simply a means to other more important ends.

Another common attribute of the professions, the skilled trades, and farming is a long period of socialization into the occupational role. The term *socialization*, as it is used by sociologists, refers to the process of learning what has to be known in order to enact a social role. The socialization process involves the acquisition of necessary skills and also a pattern of attitudes, beliefs, and values appropriate to the role. In medical school, a student learns not only medicine but also how to act like a doctor. Apprenticeship programs produce craftsmen who have learned much more than just the skills of their trade. Since almost all farmers are sons of farmers, much of their early experience represents a period of socialization into their occupation.

A long period of socialization into an occupation represents an expenditure of time and energy that increases the likelihood of an investment of "self" in the work role. And the acquisition of knowledge and skill enhances the probability of a payoff on this investment in the form of status recognition for achievement at work. Also, the social relationships occurring during the period of preparation for these occupations emphasize and reinforce the idea that occupational achievement is important. The "student" in this relationship is more or less constantly in contact with a "teacher" whose greater authority and prestige are largely occupationally based. This is clearly true of the relationship, for example, between medical students and professors and between apprentices and master craftsmen. It is also characteristic to some extent of the more complex relationship between a farmer and his sons.

The occupations in which alienation from work is least likely—the professions, skilled trades, and farming—constituted approximately one-fourth of the employed civilian labor force in 1965. Although in recent years the proportion of craftsmen has remained relatively constant and the proportion of farmers has continued to decline, professional and technical workers are the most rapidly growing segment of the labor force. It is possible that this change in the occupational composition of the labor force may eventually produce a substantial reduction of the amount of alienation from work in industrial societies. It is also possible that changes in the nature of work produced by automation may reduce the alienation experienced by semiskilled machine operators in factories and offices.[35] These possibilities will be considered in Chapter 4. At the present and probably for some time to come, however, the most common way of experiencing work in all industrial societies is likely to be alienation from it. And this widespread alienation from work has some important consequences for the character of industrial society.

The general drift toward a leisure-oriented society was described in Chapter 2. The pervasiveness of alienation from work is one of the important factors producing this pattern of change. If increasing numbers of people find that their central life interests—the activities in which they evaluate themselves and are evaluated by others—lie outside the world of work, change in the primary orientation of industrial society is inevitable. These societies have traditionally been structured around the goal of continued economic growth, with an emphasis upon raising personal-income levels. We appear to be entering a period in which time to enjoy current income is a more important value than a further increase in level of income. If the consequence is a further reduction in working hours, the overall national-income level may be lower than it would otherwise have been and energy and resources will be diverted toward meeting a growing demand for leisure products and services.

Consideration of how to allocate the benefits of increased productivity of our economy is most often framed as a choice between higher income and more leisure. There is a third alternative that merits attention. A much higher proportion of our energy and resources could be devoted to the solution of existing social problems and to preparation for meeting problems occasioned by the impending transition to an automated, postindustrial era. Some ancient and universal problems such as poverty, ignorance, disease, crime, and war persist in spite of efforts toward their eradication. Urban blight and congestion, pollution of air and water, and destruction of wilderness areas have become increasingly serious problems as a result of urbanization and population increase. The accelerating pace of social change means that solving the problems of the future may depend upon whether they have been anticipated and whether strategies for dealing with them have been developed prior to their occurrence. Solutions for present and anticipated social problems will require a much greater investment in action programs, in research, and in education. Support for research in the social sciences, from which better predictions about the outcome of social change could ensue, is small in comparison with the sum being spent on research from which technological development and accelerated social change will result. The amount being spent on public education at all levels has increased considerably, but education is still underfinanced in view of its importance in this period of transition to a new economic and social order.

Elimination of some of the oldest problems of human existence is close to being realized, and solutions for most other social problems are clearly within the realm of possibility. Solving these problems will require a substantial change in the allocation of energy and resources. Alienation from work—inherent in the social structure of mature industrial societies—has encouraged the drift toward a leisure-oriented culture and has impeded the solution of important social problems.

## Alienation and Poverty

Poverty in an otherwise affluent society is related to alienation from work and warrants special consideration in this discussion. Although industrialism has been more successful than any other cultural system in eliminating poverty, there are still many people in all industrial societies living below what are defined as minimal standards. Estimates of the number of poor vary depending upon where the poverty line is drawn; but it appears that close to one-fourth of the total population of the United States may have less-than-adequate food, shelter, and health care.[36] The adequacy of a standard of living is a relative matter, and the poor in industrial societies live at a level above most people in economically underdeveloped areas of the world. This observation does not in any way diminish the importance of poverty as a social problem in the United States. Poverty must be defined in terms of the level of living possible in societies at various stages of technological development. Focusing upon the difference between being poor in a poor society and being poor in a rich society does, however, place the issue in the context of the concerns of this book.

The social problems with which this book is concerned are those inherent in the social structure of industrial society. The existence of poverty is not a problem of this type. However, the response to poverty in mature industrial societies is mediated by the major structural attributes of these societies discussed above. To a much greater degree in industrial than in nonindustrial societies, the poor are confronted by a status-assignment system in which occupational, economic, and educational achievements are the primary basis for differentiating status levels. In an isolated peasant village where everyone is poor, poverty does not evoke a sense of personal failure: Social status is not assigned on a basis of economic criteria. Being poor in the United States poses a threat to self-esteem that requires some form of response. There was a period in the earlier stages of industrialization in this country when the most common response to poverty appears to have been a mobility orientation. The lower class was composed in large measure of immigrants who came to the

United States with the expectation of achieving upward social mobility for themselves or their children. Since that time, both the opportunity structure and the social and cultural origins of the poor have changed. The most common response to poverty today appears to be alienation.

Describing the poor as being alienated from industrialism does not, of course, mean that they prefer being poor, uneducated, and unskilled to being wealthy, well educated, or skilled. However, the likelihood of a payoff on the investment of self in the pursuit of these goals is so low that noneconomic criteria for maintaining a favorable self-image must be sought. It has become commonplace to observe that the child from a poverty background enters school with a handicap—usually referred to as "cultural deprivation"—that he may never overcome without special help. If the consequence is a low level of school achievement, the child is likely to respond by assigning a low reward value to success as a student and will drop out of school at the first opportunity. As a result he enters the labor market at a disadvantage, and the only jobs open to him will be the ones most likely to produce alienation from work.

The self-perpetuating character of poverty stemming from alienation from school and from work has led to the observation that there may be a distinct "culture of poverty." The basic assumption is that the life of the poor is ordered by a unique set of beliefs and values that does not include an emphasis upon work-related achievement. The relative isolation of the poor in rural pockets of poverty or in urban ghettos results in the transmission of the culture of poverty from one generation to the next, thereby perpetuating poverty across generations. The assumption that there is a culture of poverty has important implications for programs designed to reduce poverty: It suggests that the major focus of such programs should be upon changing the poor rather than upon changing the opportunity structure of the society.

The culture-of-poverty thesis would appear to be a more accurate description of a way in which poverty is perpetuated in isolated nonindustrial areas than of this process in the United States. Although the poor in America are isolated and have been described as "invisible" because of their limited interpersonal contacts with other segments of the society, they are clearly not insulated from exposure to the value placed upon economic achievement or from the complex set of related beliefs and assumptions that surround this value. The view presented in this chapter that the poor are alienated from industrialism in the sense that their self-esteem does not depend upon work-related achievement does not imply a culture of poverty in which a negative assessment of work is embedded. It suggests instead a specific social psychological response to a particular position in the status structure of industrial society. With appropriate changes in the opportunity structure, a mobility orientation rather than alienation would undoubtedly be the predominant response to poverty.

The fact of limited opportunity for mobility out of poverty seems incontrovertible when we examine the composition of the poor in America. Approximately one-fifth of those below the poverty line are nonwhite and subject to educational and occupational discrimination. Negro college graduates earn on the average only as much as white workers who leave school after the eighth grade. From the perspective of the Negro, Puerto Rican, or American Indian with less than a high school education, the likelihood of becoming an achiever in the world of work must seem remote indeed. Another segment of the poor with little prospect for status recognition in terms of the values of industrialism is the aged. Forty percent of the households with insufficient income in the United States are headed by people over 65. Women represent a third relatively disadvantaged category in the labor force. Almost half of all fatherless families and over half of all single women live below the poverty line.[37] Especially for women without skills or education, the likelihood of stable employment is remote. People who remain in rural depressed areas such as those that exist in the Appalachian Mountains or in the South are also unlikely to be able to sustain a commitment to the values of industrialism. Among the rural poor, the plight of the migratory laborer is particularly striking. Rural poverty, however, is perhaps more akin to the poverty found in economically underdeveloped societies, and it may not be meaningful in this instance to speak of alienation from a way of life (industrialism) in which the rural poor have never fully participated. A final major category of the economically disadvantaged is unskilled new entrants into the labor market who have less than a high school education. The problems experienced by these young people in finding employment in a rapidly changing and highly technologically developed economy was a major theme in Chapter 2.

The poor in America are clearly not a homogeneous social grouping and would appear unlikely to be participants in a common culture of poverty with all that the concept of a distinct culture implies. What they do have in common are limited marketable skills, limited education, and, for various reasons, limited prospects for moving out of their disadvantaged position. The consequence for most appears to be alienation from work and from other social roles that embody the dominant values of the industrial way of life.

## Summary

One of the most common criticisms of industrial society is the charge that it engenders shallow interpersonal relations, anonymity, apathy, and overconformity. Each of these conditions is related to the lack of commitment or identification which we have termed alienation. Alienation has been viewed in this chapter as a condition of the relationship between an individual and some social unit in which he is a participant. Specifically, it describes a condition in which the individual does not evaluate himself in terms of the criteria used for assigning status within the social unit. Under these circumstances, the individual is alienated from others in that he is unconcerned with how they evaluate him and is alienated from his self in that what he does has little relation to, or bearing upon, his self-concept.

Difficulty in affirming a positive image of self is pervasive in industrial societies. Industrial man frequently participates in activities in which he has invested little of his self and in which he is consequently self-estranged in the classic sense of this term as developed by Marx and Fromm. Freed from the bonds of small-group pre-industrial society, the individual is confronted with the problem of maintaining self-esteem in an unstable, fragmented, and poorly integrated social order. The result is a sense of powerlessness, meaninglessness, and normlessness. One consequence of experiencing the social order in these ways is a failure to invest self in social situations in which there is no certainty of a return on the investment in the form of status recognition. The effect is a disjuncture between the self-esteem maintenance and status-assignment processes. The alienation of industrial man is thus directly linked to the social structure of industrial society.

Although the problem of developing and maintaining a favorable image of self occurs throughout industrial society, there is a relationship between the intensity and frequency of alienation and position in the status structure. Alienation is a greater problem for people in lower- and working-class positions than for people in middle- and upper-class positions. The occupations in which alienation is most likely are functionally specialized unskilled or semiskilled jobs in factories and offices. The professions, the skilled trades, and farming appear to be relatively free from alienation. The major factors differentiating work roles that produce alienation from those that do not appear to be the status level of the occupation, opportunity for upward mobility, variation in the occupational-status level of work associates, the length of training time for the occupation, and the extent of integration of the work role with other areas of social experience.

Alienation from work has been the major topic of concern throughout most of this chapter. This form of alienation occupied a central place in the writing of Marx on the topic and has been the primary focus of much of the social scientific research on alienation since that time. One reason for this emphasis is the importance of the work role in industrial societies. The institutional structure of these societies is organized around the objective of continuous economic growth, and work-related values are the major determinants of social status. The centrality of the occupational role and the work organization to the industrial way of life means that alienation from work has consequences that extend far beyond the work place. One effect of increasing alienation from work might be an increasingly leisure-oriented society. The value implications of the allocation of energy and resources for leisure rather than for education, research, and the solution of social problems merit serious attention.

An additional reason for emphasizing alienation from work in this chapter is its consequences for the authority structure of organizations. An alienated work force differs from a committed work force in the type of organizational control structure it requires. In Chapter 4 this issue will be discussed in the context of a major dilemma in industrial societies: Rationalized controls are necessary, individual freedom of action is valued, and neither can be achieved without some sacrifice of the other.

# FREEDOM, CONTROL, AND THE FUTURE OF INDUSTRIAL SOCIETY

The United States has been described as an "organizational society." This description would apply equally well to any mature industrial society since the important activities within these societies are performed, for the most part, within large-scale formal organizations. Concentration of economic activity within fewer and fewer firms has gone on almost continuously since the Industrial Revolution. By 1947 the three largest American companies in automobiles, agricultural machinery, rubber tires, meat products, liquor, cigarettes, copper, tin containers, and office machinery did two-thirds or more of all business in their respective fields.[1] Today almost all major industries are dominated by a few giant corporations. Many of the workers within these industries are represented by large bureaucratically ordered unions, and the important decisions affecting these workers are increasingly made by leaders at the top of the company and union hierarchies. Centralization of authority in unions is reflected in the fact that over 80 percent of the 18 million union members in 1960 were in unions affiliated with the AFL-CIO.

The economy is not the only institution dominated by bureaucratic organizations. The largest bureaucracy of all, the United States government, has grown in only a little more than a century from under 50,000 employees to over 2 million, with a change in the Federal budget during this period of from $63 million to well over $100 billion. This change reflects not only the growth of the country but also an increasing concentration of political decision making at the Federal level.

Control of the communications industry, which has a crucial role in shaping public opinion and popular tastes in a mass society, is concentrated in a small number of firms. Only a few cities have more than one newspaper, and most are affiliated with nationwide chains. Television is dominated by three networks, radio by four networks, and the motion-picture industry by five major companies.

Religious, educational, and welfare institutions have also become more and more concentrated and bureaucratized. Congregationally based religious denominations, in which control was traditionally vested in the local congregation, have come increasingly under the sway of national or international church leadership. The process of urbanization and the growing demand for education have increased the size and organizational complexity of local school systems and universities. Greater Federal control of public-welfare activities along with the merger of private welfare agencies has led to a more concentrated control structure in eleemosynary institutions. Even the family has become bureaucratized in the sense that many of the functions performed by this institution in preindustrial society—education, work, and religious observance—are now performed outside the family in large formal organizations.

Robert Presthus has summarized the emergence of bureaucracy as a major organizational form in our society as follows:

Beginning about 1875, social, economic, and political trends in the United States prepared the way for the "organizational society," characterized by large-scale bureaucratic institutions in practically every major social area. The major trends included the separation of ownership from management; increasing size and concentration in business, industry, and even eleemosynary fields; the decline of competition; the development of a political economy; and the emergence of an *employee* society.[2]

The significance for our concerns of the fact that industrial societies are organizational societies is twofold. First, while the primary functions of formal organizations in American society are varied, they are all *work* organizations. It is for this reason that Presthus describes the United States as an employee society. If the control of industrial society rests mainly in large-scale organizations and if a majority of the employees of these organizations are alienated from work as suggested in the preceding chapter, the type of organizational authority structure necessitated by an alienated work force has an important bearing upon the exercise of power in industrial societies. One focus of concern in this chapter will be upon the relationship between alienation and social control.

A second theme in this chapter will be the dilemma posed by the inability to maximize both freedom and control in societies dominated by formal organizations. The value placed upon preserving individual freedom of action has a long history in Western civilization. The amount of control necessary for a highly differentiated and poorly integrated social order to function, however, necessarily abridges this freedom. The existence of a rationalized control structure in organizational societies poses other important value questions regarding the appropriate directions for planned change.

In this chapter we shall consider first the ways in which alienation from work affects the exercise of authority in formal organizations. We shall then discuss the implications of the bureaucratic system of authority for the general dilemma of freedom versus control, and we shall conclude the chapter with an analysis of the ways in which automation may change the social structure of industrial society. Some of the value questions posed by the transition to postindustrial society will be included in this discussion.

### Alienation and Social Control

Social control refers to the process through which the behavior of individual members of a social unit becomes consistent with the norms defining what is appropriate behavior within that unit. The location of the controls at the point at which they affect behavior may be either internal or external to the individual. When we speak of internal social control we mean that the individual has learned what is expected of him in the various social roles that he plays and has acquired the skills and the motivation to meet these expectations. One of the major points in Chapter 3 was that motivation to meet social expectations or to achieve shared goals is dependent upon some degree of correspondence between the ways in which the individual evaluates himself and the ways in which he is evaluated by others. A person is motivated to act in socially prescribed ways, at least in part, because in so doing he acquires social status which confirms a favorable image of self. Effective internal controls, then, are dependent upon (1) a clearly defined and consensually held set of norms defining appropriate behavior, (2) individuals who have learned their social roles and who have acquired the skill needed to perform them, and (3) individuals who are committed to, rather than alienated from, the social unit within which the norms are shared.

These three conditions are much more common in small face-to-face social units such as families or nonindustrial villages than they are in larger and more complex social units. Even in families or villages, external controls are necessary in order to produce the socialization of the young, of the novice, or of the stranger (condition 2 above). A system of external controls involves a superordinate-subordinate relationship, in which one party to the relationship establishes the definition of what is appropriate and administers rewards and punishments designed to produce compliance with the definition. This type of social control becomes necessary whenever any of the three conditions that permit internal controls is not met. In general, we would expect a preponderance of external social controls in industrial societies. The relatively low level of social structuring characteristic of these societies means that norms are not clearly defined, and a high level of structural differentiation reduces the likelihood of consensus regarding definitions of appropriate behavior.

Our concern at this point is specifically with the control structure of formal organizations, and in social units of this type, conditions 1 and 2 above are both likely to be met. Rationalized role definitions in the form of job descriptions provide a clear specification of what members of an organization are supposed to do, while selective recruitment and training programs produce knowledge of job requirements and the skills needed to perform them.

What may be missing is a sufficient commitment to work and to the work organization for internal constraints to be an effective means of social control. Functionally specialized and low-skilled jobs produce alienation from work and indifference toward organizational goals. The conditions producing work alienation described in Chapter 3 are most often found in combination in large-scale formal organizations. Presthus arrives at a similar conclusion regarding work in a bureaucratic setting:

Indifference is the typical pattern of accommodation for the majority of organization men. The indifferents are found among the great mass of waged and salaried employees who work in the bureaucratic situation. In 1960 such employees comprised almost ninety per cent of the labor force, divided almost equally into blue- and white-collar workers. By a very rough estimate, we can say that some twenty-five million of them, just about half the wage-earning labor force, now work in big organizations. . . . It is not to be inferred that all of these employees are indifferents, nor can anyone determine the number who are. Both logic and empirical research, however, suggest that a considerable proportion of them have been alienated by the structural conditions of big organization. . . .[3]

The thesis proposed here is that bureaucracy is essentially a system of external controls that has developed in response to the problem of controlling an alienated work force. The term *bureaucracy* has been used to describe a wide variety of attributes of complex, formal organizations. At the core of the concept is the idea of a hierarchical authority structure with multiple levels of supervision. Max Weber, in the classical analysis of the development of bureaucracy, describes several characteristics of bureaucracies in addition to hierarchical authority: fixed and official jurisdictional areas, administration based on written documents, expertly trained managers, and management through stable general rules.[4] The emphasis in his analysis of the emergence of bureaucracy is upon the development of hierarchical authority in a rational-legal framework. Some recent studies of formal organizations have indicated that bureaucratic administration can be distinguished from rational administration and that the two do not always appear together.[5] The major element defining bureaucratic administration in these studies is a hierarchy of authority, whereas elements of rational administration include a work force with specialized competence, rewards for performance based upon contributions to the organization, and contractual agreements defining goals and responsibilities.

In the most common explanation for the emergence of bureaucracy, it is seen as a response to the problem of administering increasingly large and complex organizations. In the context of the distinction made above between bureaucratic and rationalized administrative procedures, however, the problems associated with size and complexity are most directly responsible for the *rationalization* of organizational structure and procedures. Bureaucratic controls, on the other hand, may be more closely related to problems in the supervision of alienated employees.

If the essence of bureaucracy is a hierarchy composed of many levels of supervision, what sort of organization requires a control structure of this sort? Very little social scientific research has been directed toward an answer to this question. There have been studies that identify certain occupations for which bureaucratic controls are apparently unnecessary. There is a considerable amount of recent research, for example, demonstrating that the professions are characterized by a control structure that is fundamentally different from the hierarchical control exercised in bureaucracies.[6] Control in the professions is centered in the professional association which establishes standards of competence and certifies that members of the profession have met these standards. Professionals thus have a clearly defined set of norms regulating their conduct; they have a long period of training leading to certification of their skill; and as noted in Chapter 3; they are strongly committed to, rather than alienated from, work. For these reasons, internal controls are effective and close supervision is not needed.

Professionals are increasingly employed in large organizations, and most of the studies cited above have been concerned with the conflict between professional and bureaucratic administrative considerations. The finding that such conflict exists is evidence in support of the contention that professional and bureaucratic control structures are incompatible. It is important to note, however, that many other attributes of large formal organizations—notably rationality—are not at all incompatible with professional patterns of behavior. As Peter Blau and Richard Scott point out, among the aspects of complex organizations, "only disciplined compliance with orders of hierarchical superiors entails a fundamental conflict with professionalism."[7] It is the imposition of a system of external organizational constraints upon an occupational group for whom internal controls are sufficient that poses the problem.

A second occupational group for whom close supervision is unnecessary is the skilled trades. The skilled worker has internalized standards of workmanship and an identification with, or commitment to, his craft. As in the case with the professions, there are a prolonged period of training and formal certification of competence. Stinchcombe, in the study mentioned previously, demonstrates, for example, that the construction industry is not bureaucratically administered. He states that "administration in the construction industry depends upon a highly professionalized manual labor force" and that "the professionalization of the labor force in the construction industry serves the same functions as bureaucratic administration in mass production industries."[8] Skilled workers comprise a large proportion of the work force in the construction industry, and craft institutions are adequate for social control of the work process.

It is important to note, with regard to the general thesis we are developing, that technical socialization and certified competence—attributes of both the professions and the skilled trades—are not in themselves sufficient to obviate the necessity for external controls. Skill in the absence of a commitment to the job and to the work organization provides no guarantee of effective performance of the work role. A long period of socialization into a professional or skilled occupation, however, militates against alienation from work; and it is the alienated worker for whom bureaucratic supervision is most appropriate.

The idea that autonomy on the job is feasible only for employees who are not alienated from work reverses the direction of the relationship customarily noted between alienation and control. Many studies have demonstrated that alienated workers are most often found in jobs in which they have little autonomy or control over the decisions that affect their work. The assumption in these studies is that lack of autonomy produces alienation. Robert Blauner, in his comparative analysis of alienation in the chemical, printing, textile, and automobile industries, found that social alienation was highest in the latter two industries, in which workers have little freedom or autonomy.[9] An example of a different sort can be found in contemporary management theory. One of the major elements of this theory is "participative management," in which it is assumed that by giving workers a larger role in decision-making processes within their organization, alienation is lessened and productivity increased.

Although the emphasis in this chapter is upon the ways in which bureaucratic controls are rendered necessary by an alienated work force, it should not be inferred that the cause-and-effect relationship occurs only in this direction. In fact, there appears to be a circular or reciprocally reinforcing relationship between alienation and bureaucratization. Alienation from work necessitates a bureaucratic control structure which engenders further alienation from work which encourages stricter bureaucratic controls. Chris Argyris, who has written extensively on the relation between individuals and organizations, has expressed a similar view of this process. The following quotation is taken from a list of basic propositions in his theory.

Individuals will adapt to frustration and conflict [in formal organizations] by creating any one of a combination of the following informal activities:

1. Leave the situation (absenteeism and turnover).
2. Climb the organizational ladder.
3. Become defensive (daydream, become aggressive, develop grievances, regress, project grievances, feel a low sense of self-worth).
4. Become apathetic, disinterested, non-ego-involved in the organization and its formal goals.

5. Create informal groups to sanction the defense reactions in (3) and (4).
6. Formalize the informal groups in the form of trade unions.
7. De-emphasize the importance of self-growth, creativity, and so forth and emphasize the importance of money and other material rewards.
8. Accept the ways of behaving outlined above as being proper for their life outside the organization.

Management will tend to view most of the informal activities as detrimental to the formal organization. They will tend to resist the informal activities by tightening the formal organization structure, increasing the directive leadership and the managerial controls.

Such reactions will tend to increase the employees' subordination, which in turn will increase their frustration, failure, and similar reactions, which in turn will increase the informal activities. Thus one has a circular process in seemingly perpetual motion.[10]

Thus far we have emphasized the idea that bureaucratization is a *management* response to the problem of controlling an alienated work force. There is some evidence that alienated workers *prefer* a system of external controls so long as it is neither repressive nor arbitrary. The exercise of internal controls requires involvement in decision making and personal responsibility for decisions that are made. A worker who is not ego-involved in his job and who is indifferent toward the achievement of organizational goals may seek to avoid precisely this kind of responsibility. Argyris's finding that alienated industrial workers express a need "to be left alone" and "to be passive" in their work is typical of the results of many studies in this area.[11] A related research finding that has also been repeatedly demonstrated is that most industrial workers do not aspire to be foremen because they do not want the responsibility involved in this position.

The pattern of preference for an externally controlled work environment is by no means limited to blue-collar workers. Since alienation from work extends into many white-collar occupations as well, we would expect to find a similar set of values regarding social control in these occupations. For white-collar workers in large, complex organizations, control is more a matter of adherence to rules and regulations than of personal supervision of the sort found in the foreman-worker relationship. *Overconformity* to these rules represents abdication of personal responsibility—that is, of internal controls—in favor of external control mechanisms. Zealous compliance with regulations accompanied by the comment, "I don't make the rules," is a common pattern in bureaucracies at all but the highest administrative levels. This pattern is perhaps most typical of military organizations, in which "passing the buck" is standard operating procedure. A case in point is the difficulty encountered at the Nuremberg trials following World War II in fixing responsibility for war crimes. The standard defense at these trials was that the accused was only following orders.

This decline in what Mannheim termed "substantial rationality" represents a decline in the efficacy of internal controls and is related, as we noted in Chapter 3, to alienation from work. Robert Merton describes overconformity to regulations as the major attribute of what he calls the "bureaucratic personality."[12] These observations indicate the widespread reliance upon external controls in industrial society and suggest that these controls are not imposed upon an unwilling work force. The bureaucratic control structure not only serves a function for management in ensuring work-role performance but also serves the need of alienated blue- and white-collar workers to avoid personal responsibility in an area in which they have invested little of themselves.

In Chapter 3, Erich Fromm's analysis of the process of individuation and the development of freedom from small-group controls was summarized. Fromm makes a distinction between "freedom from," or negative freedom and "freedom to," or positive freedom, and this distinction is relevant to our concerns in this chapter. The freeing of the individual from the constraints of traditional authority represents negative freedom in Fromm's terms. Positive freedom refers to the "full realization of the individual's potentialities, together with his ability to live actively and spontaneously."[13] Achieving "freedom to," in other words, involves the exercise of internal controls rather than reliance upon external controls and also requires an investment of self in activities that provide opportunity for self-realization. In the period since the Renaissance, negative freedom has become common in Western civilization; but the attainment of freedom in its positive sense is still rare. The result, according to Fromm, is aloneness, insecurity, and anxiety. One pattern of "escape from freedom" is the submersion of self in totalitarian social or political movements which serve as the functional equivalent of traditional authority. Fromm indicates that this process may account for the popularity of the Nazi party in pre-World War II Germany.[14] A similar process may be involved today in the appeal of nationalism and nationalist parties for people in developing nations where traditional cultures are disintegrating. This process may also help to explain the willingness of alienated blue- and white-collar workers in mature industrial societies to submit to hierarchical, bureaucratic controls.

To summarize, technological developments beginning with the Industrial Revolution, along with the widespread application of the organizational principle of functional specialization, have produced a great many narrowly defined and low-skilled jobs in industrial economies. For reasons detailed in Chapter 3, jobs of this kind have had the effect of alienating a substantial proportion of the labor force in industrial societies. Increasing bureaucratization of organizational control structures has developed, in part, as a response to the problem of controlling an alienated work force. Hierarchical authority, specific rules and regulations, and narrow spans of control serve the organizational objective of ensuring that work is performed according to job specifications. An elaborate system of external controls is also consistent with the need of alienated blue- and white-collar workers to minimize their responsibilities in an area of low ego-involvement. Lack of autonomy in bureaucratically regulated jobs thus reinforces the alienative potential of functionally specialized work roles.

To what extent is alienation from work and the surrender of individual initiative and responsibility to a bureaucratic control system a social problem? It might be argued that the withdrawal of ego-involvement from an activity that offers little prospect for self-realization or self-esteem is an adaptive rather than a maladaptive response. Robert Dubin has suggested that the concern expressed by social analysts with limited opportunities for self-realization in the work role may be misplaced. He states that "self realization may be a matter of indifference to people for whom work is not a 'central life interest.' Their self-realization comes in other institutional settings outside the productive institution."[15] A major point in Chapter 3 was that work is only one of a wide variety of settings in a structurally differentiated society in which self-esteem "testing" can occur; moreover, the self-identity in the work role *need not be* an evaluated identity. The primary intent of Chapter 3 was not only to explain the widespread apathy and indifference toward work in industrial society but also to correct the common misconception that work is *necessarily* the primary or only arena for self-evaluation and self-realization.

People who are unable to derive a satisfactory self-image from the work role will seek to do so in other areas of social experience. We can now raise the question of how successful they are in this quest. The available evidence indicates that while some alienated workers find satisfying and self-actualizing experiences off the job, a great many others do not. This evidence supports our contention that creative, status-producing work is not *essential* to the process of self-realization and suggests that the development of skill in the use of time away from work may be a viable alternative to the impossible task of providing self-actualizing work experiences for everyone. This same evidence also indicates, however, that most alienated workers may not have these skills and that some important social problems may be related to alienation from work.

We shall first discuss the effects upon the individual of alienation and of reliance upon external controls and then consider some of the consequences for industrial societies. Chris Argyris has been one of the most persistent critics of the effects of formal organizations upon their members. He sees a fundamental lack of congruence between the needs of individuals and the needs of organizations. His conception of the needs of individuals is based, in large part, upon the work of the psychologist A. H. Maslow. Maslow suggests that "lower-order" needs, such as physiological needs, safety, and security, must be satisfied at least to some degree before such "higher-order" needs as self-respect, respect from others, and autonomy can be attended to. The highest-order need is self-actualization, by which he means the desire for self-fulfillment or for becoming "everything that one is capable of becoming." Psychological health and maturity are dependent upon the satisfaction of higher-order needs, but it is particularly these needs, according to Argyris, that are incongruent with the structure of formal organizations. Argyris emphasizes particularly the ways in which task specialization and hierarchical control block the development of maturity, by which he means principally a reliance upon internal controls. Specifically, Argyris identifies the following growth trends as movements in the direction of self-actualization and maturity:

1. . . . from a state of passivity as infants to a state of increasing activity as adults.
2. . . . from a state of dependence upon others as infants to a state of relative independence as adults.
3. . . . from being capable of behaving only in a few ways as an infant to being capable of behaving in many different ways as an adult.
4. . . . from having erratic, casual, shallow, quickly-dropped interests as an infant to having deeper interests as an adult.
5. . . . from having a short time perspective (i.e., the present largely determines behavior) as an infant to a much longer time perspective as an adult (i.e., where the behavior is more affected by the past and the future).
6. . . . from being in a subordinate position in the family and society as an infant to aspiring to occupy an equal and/or superordinate position relative to their peers.
7. . . . from a lack of awareness of self as an infant to an awareness of and control over self as an adult.[16]

The relevance of these dimensions of growth to our concern with workers who are alienated and who accept dependence upon an externally administered system of organizational controls is that their behavior at work falls toward the less "mature" end of each of these dimensions. The important question in terms of general personality growth and development, however, is whether this "immature" (in Argyris's terms) behavior on the job carries over into non-work-related areas of experience. In other words, does the orientation toward authority in the work organization which is produced by alienation from work limit the development of a "mature" orientation toward authority in general? Although the evidence on this point is far from conclusive, it does suggest that the alienated worker may be more generally reliant upon external controls.

Alienation and the absence of inner-directedness appear to have a general effect upon a person's satisfaction with life and upon his mental health. Although few studies have dealt specifically with this effect, there are many studies from which it could be inferred. Research comparing the general level of social and psychological adjustment of people in occupations varying in alienative potential permits the inference that alienation from work is one of the factors producing differences that are observed. As an illustration of the findings from research of this kind, we shall review the results of a recent study by Arthur Kornhauser dealing with the mental health of industrial workers.[17] In this study intensive interviews were conducted with a sample of 407 automobile workers and with a sample of 298 workers in other occupations and industries for purposes of comparison. The outstanding finding of the study was that mental health varies consistently with the skill level of jobs; a much larger proportion of skilled workers than of unskilled workers had high mental health scores. After analyzing many factors that might account for this difference, Kornhauser concludes that "by far the most influential attribute is the opportunity the work offers—or fails to offer— for use of the worker's abilities and for associated feelings of interest, sense of accomplishment, personal growth, and self-respect."[18] This finding indicates that alienation from work, in the sense in which we have been using the term, may be important in determining level of mental health.

It was suggested earlier in this chapter that there is a reciprocally reinforcing relationship between alienation and bureaucratic controls. Data from Kornhauser's study indicate that there may be at least an additive effect of these two factors upon mental health. Mental health of automobile workers varies with size of plant, and the presumably more alienated unskilled workers have particularly poor mental health only in very large plants in which we would expect a higher level of impersonal bureaucratic controls. Less rigid and more personal supervision in smaller plants may mitigate somewhat the influence of low-skilled and specialized tasks.

There are also data from this study that bear directly upon the question of whether alienated workers find satisfying and ego-gratifying activities off the job. It is clear that some automobile workers are able to do so. The differences, for example, between skilled and low-skilled workers in general satisfaction with life are much narrower than the differences in satisfaction with their jobs. Since the narrowing of the range is accounted for primarily by the fact that low-skilled workers are more satisfied with life in general than they are with their jobs, it can be assumed that compensatory non-work-related experiences for these workers are what make the difference. These data are summarized in Table 9.

**TABLE 9.    Comparison of Automobile Workers' Job Satisfaction and Satisfaction with Life**

| Type of worker | Percent "high" on job-satisfaction index | Percent satisfied with life |
|---|---|---|
| Skilled | 72 (176)* | 70 (174) |
| Repetitive semiskilled | 35 (103) | 60 (103) |

* Figures in parentheses represent the number of workers on which the percentages are based.

SOURCE: Based upon Table 5-1, p. 85, and Table 9-1, p. 187, in Arthur Kornhauser, *Mental Health of the Industrial Worker,* John Wiley & Sons, Inc., New York, 1965. Data for young and middle-aged workers, which were separated in the original tables, have been combined in the table above.

Satisfaction with life is undoubtedly related to the ability to maintain a favorable image of self. It is clear from the data in the table above that low-skilled workers are more likely than skilled workers to maintain self-esteem in terms of non-work-related self-identities and that some are successful in doing so. It should be noted, however, that 40 percent of the low-skilled workers express something less than satisfaction with life, and this may reflect difficulties in self-esteem maintenance. The assumptions made in Chapter 3 that people seek to maintain a favorable self-image, that this is a selective process, and that work is only one of a variety of institutional settings in which it may occur do not mean that people who withdraw ego-involvement from work are *automatically* successful when they reinvest it elsewhere. The same personal attributes and environmental characteristics that affect level of commitment to work can be expected to affect commitment to non-work-related activities. It is skill in a status-producing activity that is crucial for self-esteem maintenance. It appears that many of the people who are alienated from work are also less likely to have acquired interests and skills that could be used to acquire social status off the job. Active participation in community affairs, for example, is a genuine alternative to work as a basis for social honor in most communities. In a study of a small town in Michigan it was found that the social status of people depended *more* upon whether they were active in community organizations than upon the nature of their work.[19] This study, Kornhauser's study, and many others indicate that participation in community activities is much more common for people in high-status occupations than for people in low-status occupations.

Although 60 percent of the low-skilled automobile workers in Kornhauser's study express satisfaction with life, only 21 percent score high on his index of mental health. If we assume that good mental health requires a favorable image of self, it is apparent that some workers report being satisfied with life in spite of not being satisfied with themselves. Satisfaction with life may result from the achievement of goals that are set too low to be recognized as an achievement by others. Where this is the case, attaining goals that make life satisfactory will still not permit confirmation of a favorable self-image. The off-the-job activities that contribute to satisfaction with life may also not be activities that involve self-realizing or self-actualizing experiences. Although it is apparently possible to be satisfied with a life devoid of these experiences, they are essential to the development of self-esteem and consequently necessary for good mental health.

Based upon the data we have reported and other findings from his study, Kornhauser arrives at the following conclusion regarding the relationship between work and life away from the job:

Instead of merely suppressing or abandoning goals, men may *redefine* their aims; they may develop alternative, more appropriate goals toward which they can strive with a sense of worthwhile accomplishment and genuine satisfaction. Our research reveals many instances of this process—for example, when workers in jobs devoid of intrinsic interest focus instead on extrinsic rewards like wages and security; or when they turn to self-actualizing, creative hobbies away from the job to take the place of what is unattainable at work. To some extent, that is, industrial workers maintain their mental health by adapting their wants to available opportunities for gratification.

Our results indicate, however, that most workers are not too successful in this regard; we have repeatedly had to note not only deficiencies of motivation and enjoyment in work but also the relative barrenness of leisure-time interests and the restricted character of life aims. Given the structure of wants and expectations that our culture typically instills into workers, there is little tendency for them to develop other aims that might better fit their situation and better contribute to mental health.[20]

To summarize, although employed persons in industrial societies spend approximately one-third of their waking hours each week at work, many of these persons are alienated from work and most are employed by complex formal organizations. Alienation from work encourages reliance upon external organizational controls; people who are alienated may prefer to have rules, regulations, and supervisors to tell them what to do on the job so long as the rules are not arbitrary and the supervision not repressive. Excessive reliance upon external controls at work produces a generally passive, apathetic, and non-purposive life-style.[21] Habits of commitment, identification, and inner-direction may not develop or may atrophy if the work role provides no opportunity for their use. While there are realistic alternatives to the work role on which to base self-esteem and in which to achieve self-realization, taking advantage of these opportunities requires an active and purposeful orientation toward life. A positive attitude toward self is dependent upon opportunities for the actualization of potential abilities in status-producing activities, and both self-esteem and self-realization are critical components of good mental health.

The mental health problems associated with alienation and lack of inner-direction are reflected in the fact that there is a higher incidence of psychotic and neurotic conditions among people in lower-status occupations. Apart from these more severe problems, there are large differences in the general quality of human existence in industrial societies that center on the extent to which people have an active and purposeful orientation toward life. The nature of jobs in industrial societies, including many that extend well up the occupational-status hierarchy, in combination with the nature of bureaucratic work organizations makes it unlikely that a purposive life-style will develop around intrinsically work-related goals. Off-the-job activities such as status-producing patterns of consumption, creative hobbies, or participation in community affairs may provide satisfactory alternative goals. Alienation from work and habitual reliance upon external controls, however, decrease the likelihood of a commitment to non-work-related as well as to work-related goals.

Some authors have argued that the informal activities of people on the job—the non-work-related interpersonal relationships with fellow workers—mitigate to some extent the effects of work in an impersonal bureaucratic setting. There is considerable evidence from industrial sociological studies that satisfying social relations on the job relieves monotony and contributes to job satisfaction. At least for people in lower-status occupations, however, these social relations seldom extend beyond the work place; industrial workers rarely get together with their coworkers off the job. This fact as well as the effect of turnover and transfer rates upon the stability of work-group composition make social status (and consequently self-esteem) derived from activities in the work group transitory and limited to the work place. Also, the content of these activities is unlikely to generate either a sense of self-realization or longer-range goals and a purposive life-style.

It is possible that changes which are beginning to occur in management practices will help to resolve these problems; job-enlargement plans may decrease alienation from work, and participative management may provide more autonomy and force the exercise of internal controls. There has been a significant change in the orientation of American management since the days of Frederick Taylor and the "Scientific Management Movement" in the early decades of this century. Douglas McGregor, one of the major spokesmen for the new managerial policies and practices, has contrasted the assumptions underlying traditional organizations, which he calls Theory X, with those underlying newer policies, which he refers to as Theory Y. The assumptions of Theory Y, which are essentially the opposite of Theory X, are as follows:

1. *The expenditure of physical and mental effort in work is as natural as play or rest.* The average human being does not inherently dislike work. Depending upon controllable conditions, work may be a source of satisfaction (and will be voluntarily performed) or a source of punishment (and will be avoided if possible).

2. *External control and the threat of punishment are not the only means for bringing about effort toward organizational objectives. Man will exercise self-direction and self-control in the service of objectives to which he is committed.*

3. *Commitment to objectives is a function of the rewards associated with their achievement.* The most significant of such rewards, e.g., the satisfaction of ego and self-actualization needs, can be direct products of effort directed toward organizational objectives.

4. *The average human being learns, under proper conditions, not only to accept but to seek responsibility.* Avoidance of responsibility, lack of ambition, and emphasis on security are generally consequences of experience, not inherent human characteristics.

5. *The capacity to exercise a relatively high degree of imagination, ingenuity, and creativity in the solution of organizational problems is widely, not narrowly, distributed in the population.*

6. *Under the conditions of modern industrial life, the intellectual potentialities of the average human being are only partially utilized.*[22]

The relevance of these assumptions to our concern with alienation and control is clear. Management based upon the assumptions of Theory Y would lead to job enlargement rather than job specialization and to freedom and autonomy on the job rather than restrictive, bureaucratic controls. Widespread implementation of these practices could break the vicious circle between alienation from work and external social control and could lead to an organizational environment that would be more consistent with basic human needs.

It is doubtful, however, that this will happen. Although advocacy of Theory Y is common among the intellectual spokesmen for American management, the vast majority of organizations are administered on a basis of assumptions much closer to Theory X. One important reason this is so is that managers and administrators are understandably reluctant to modify the division of labor or the control structure of an organization that is successful. And almost all large-scale organizations are to some degree successful. There have been relatively few instances of unprofitable operation of large business and industrial concerns during the past several decades. Furthermore, although it is more difficult to measure the success of nonprofit organizations, most appear to be achieving their immediate objectives. *A committed work force is not a condition for success of bureaucratically ordered organizations*; with supervision and explicit rules and regulations, employees will perform their specialized tasks whether or not they have any ego invested in them.

Both evidence and logic suggest that organizations would be even more successful if they were structured in such a way as to encourage self-esteem maintenance and self-actualization on the job. But changing an organization that is already operating with some degree of success always involves risk. And the bureaucrat in mature industrial societies is much less inclined to take risks than the entrepreneur in early industrial societies. Minimizing the possibility of failure appears to be a more common objective today than maximizing the possibility of success. For this reason, there is resistance to organizational change; job-enlargement and participative-management schemes have not been generally applied in the large organizations in which most of the affairs of industrial society are conducted.

Even where these practices have been tried, they have not always been designed in a way that would significantly reduce alienation or increase autonomy. Job-enlargement plans often involve simply the combination of several specialized tasks into one job, as would be the case, for example, if an automobile assembler responsible for mounting the rearview mirror were given the additional tasks of inserting the speedometer and attaching the glove-compartment door. Modifying jobs in this way may make them less monotonous but does not make them more meaningful, nor does it increase the level of skill ships. Any basic change in the relation of men to machines is likely skill and responsibility that permit ego-involvement or commitment to work. Although there have been some exceptions, notably the restructuring of jobs that has occurred in several IBM plants, most job-enlargement plans have been designed with the intention of reducing monotony rather than of decreasing alienation from work. Similarly, participative management plans do not always involve workers in the important decisions that affect their jobs. Delegation of responsibility for inconsequential decisions is not likely to increase autonomy or to decrease the worker's sense of powerlessness. At worst, participative management is a manipulative device designed to secure cooperation by making people think they have participated in a decision that, in fact, had already been made. Even at best, participative management can have only a limited effect in organizations characterized by a high level of job specialization. The degree of division of labor largely determines the importance of decisions to be made within any segment of an organization. For this reason, effective participation in decision making may often require an accompanying plan for significant job enlargement. This procedure not only would ensure that the decisions to be made are of some consequence but also would increase commitment to work and, consequently, would produce greater worker concern with involvement in the decision-making process.

Management resistance to change is not the only factor limiting the spread or the effectiveness of practices based upon Theory Y. The nature of industrial technology places some limits upon the ways in which organizational structure can be changed. Extensive division of labor and a man-machine relationship in which skill is built into the machine are, to some extent, inherent in industrial technology. However, there are possibilities for creating more meaningful jobs through technological change that have been largely ignored. Creating a work environment in industrial societies that is as consistent as possible with basic human needs requires attention to these needs in the engineering as well as the management of industrial organizations.

Georges Friedmann sees the development of job-enlargement plans as a reversal of the traditional pattern of continuous increase in job specialization, and he describes the change as the "decline of an orthodoxy."[23] Douglas McGregor, while noting that the assumptions of Theory X are predominant today, states that a possible result of the adoption of new management theories could be "developments during the next few decades with respect to the human side of enterprise comparable to those that have occurred in technology during the past half century."[24] Technological constraints and management reluctance to change would seem to dictate a less optimistic view of the effects of new policies and practices in organizational administration. This does not mean that we should ignore whatever possibilities these techniques may offer for reducing the conflict between organizational and human needs. It does suggest that eliminating alienation and reliance upon external controls may require fundamental changes in the technology and social structure of industrial society—changes that would signal the advent of a new postindustrial social order. The possible impact of automation upon the future of industrial society will be discussed later in this chapter. We shall first, however, consider some additional ways in which the control structure of industrial society may shape its future.

## Freedom and Control

The idea that "eternal vigilance is the price of liberty" has been a common theme in political speeches since the eighteenth century. The threat to liberty with which these orators are most often concerned comes from hostile foreign nations or from "foreign" ideologies. Political scientists, more often than political orators, are concerned with another kind of threat to individual freedom—one which is internal and inherent in the social structure of industrial society. The contention that the greatest danger to liberty is built into the structure of our society, which will be the primary concern of this section, may at first seem paradoxical. The social structural changes accompanying industrialization freed the individual from small-group constraints in a fixed social order, and democratic political institutions are more often found today in industrial than in nonindustrial societies.

If the threat to freedom from within industrial society is seen as a paradox, most of the other social problems with which we have been concerned in this book may also seem paradoxical: We have spoken of overconformity in a society that tolerates a wide range of behavior, even with regard to such fundamental issues as whether one marries and whether one works. We have spoken of apathy and lack of an active and purposeful life in a society whose members, by contrast to peasant villagers, are strongly goal-oriented. We have spoken of the surrender of aspirations for occupational achievement in a type of society with higher rates of upward social mobility than any other in history. Conformity, apathy, loss of achievement motivation, and abridgment of individual freedom are nevertheless important social problems in industrial society.

The paradoxical nature of this assertion disappears if we consider again what is meant by a *social* problem. In Chapter 1 a social problem was defined as a "situation believed to be a threat to or an infringement upon an established social value and considered capable of amelioration or elimination by appropriate social action." Preservation of individual freedom is one of the major social values of industrial society, and we have higher aspirations with regard to the level of freedom our society *should* permit than are held in most nonindustrial societies. Industrial man also has greater faith than the serf in a medieval manor or the peasant in a contemporary village in the efficacy of social action as a means of dealing with the infringement of freedom. And by the standards of freedom we apply, the structure of industrial society constitutes a threat to freedom requiring "eternal vigilance."

The attributes of our society that infringe upon individual freedom and produce conformity, apathy, and loss of achievement motivation are the same attributes that make freedom, self-actualization, commitment, and aspirations for upward mobility possible. It is only in societies characterized by a high level of structural differentiation, a relative lack of structural integration, and an open class system that men may reasonably aspire to these goals. Unless attainment of a goal is perceived as possible, its absence is unlikely to be defined as a problem. Specifically with regard to individual freedom, the process of individuation, beginning with the Renaissance and greatly accelerated by the Industrial Revolution, was a necessary prelude to the contemporary concern with liberty as a right of all members of society. Freedom is not a meaningful concept unless there are important choices to be made; and in nonindustrial cultures, the range of alternatives in important areas of life is very restricted. The process of achieving "freedom from," as described by Fromm, involves the shift of responsibility for important decisions to the individual and away from traditional cultural prescriptions enforced by small-group controls. In a stable and undifferentiated society, people are what they have learned to be and are seldom confronted with the possibility that they might become anything other than what they are. Industrial man in a changing and highly differentiated society is constantly exposed to the *possibility* of choice because every day he sees people who have made choices that were apparently different from his own. Whatever abridges his ability to choose among alternatives may be perceived as a threat to his freedom.

Although individual freedom may not be a meaningful issue in small-group-controlled societies where the individual is not the agent of choice, it does not follow that maximum freedom exists in the total absence of social controls. Complete anarchy is not the ideal condition for freedom of choice. It does represent the extreme of what Fromm calls negative freedom but is not the best condition for the purposive self-actualizing choices that represent positive freedom. Freedom of this sort requires shared or socially defined goals and a system of social controls that protects the right of each individual to pursue these goals. The guarantees of civil liberties that are built into democratic political systems, for example, are essential to the achievement of positive freedom but are a form of social control.[25]

Attainment of positive freedom is most likely with some *optimum* balance of individual freedom and social control. This idea is not at all new. John Stuart Mill wrote in the nineteenth century, "The practical question [is] where to place the limit—how to make the fitting adjustment between individual independence and social control."[26] Although it has been approximately 100 years since this was written, we appear to be no closer to arriving at a formula for making "the fitting adjustment." Meanwhile, the balance between freedom and control has been affected in important ways by the events of the past century.

The most serious threats to individual freedom come from unrestrained conflict, unresolved social problems, chaos, and disorder. Wherever these conditions exist, the response is most likely to be an increase in both the level and the centralization of social control. The autocratic governments in most newly developed nations in Africa and Asia, where traditional societies have been disrupted and extensive rational-legal controls not yet established, are cases in point. The greater governmental control of the United States economy growing out of the Depression of the 1930s, when as much as one-fourth of the labor force was unemployed, is an illustration of the same process. The special powers granted to heads of state during time of war is another example and a particularly important one, since the threat of global atomic war has existed more or less continuously throughout the past two decades.

Internal conflict and disorder are more characteristic of early than of mature industrial societies. In the later stages of industrialization, a complex web of rules develops which serves to mediate conflict and prevent chaos and disorder. In Western industrial nations, industrialization occurred over a long period of time and within the context of a set of values emphasizing individual freedom. This combination of events helped to ensure the development of democratic political institutions. In the developing nations of the world today, industrialization is occurring at a more rapid pace; the threat of internal conflict and chaos is greater; and moreover, manufacturing industries are being introduced as a program of *planned* change. The planning of a transformation as basic as the shift from an agricultural to an industrial society demands a high level of centralized control. In these nations, the value placed upon individual freedom is in conflict with the value placed upon rapid economic growth and the elimination of poverty. As a result of the "revolution of rising expectations" throughout the economically underdeveloped areas of the world, freedom may be seen as a less immediate and important goal than adequate food, shelter, and clothing. Furthermore, it does not appear that autocratic governments in these areas, so long as they are successful in stimulating economic growth, are imposed against the will of the people. This observation is consistent with Maslow's hypothesis that lower-order needs—hunger, for example—must be satisfied before concern develops with higher-order needs such as freedom. If this is true, it may help to explain the difference in the balance between freedom and control that has been established in the older industrial nations and that in the newly developing ones including the Soviet Union, which has achieved its present level of economic development in less than fifty years.

Although the more dramatic threats to individual freedom occur during the early stages of industrialization, there are constant, less obvious, and therefore more insidious pressures to change the balance of freedom and control in mature industrial societies. If we conceive of freedom in the very broad sense that Fromm intends when he speaks of positive freedom, those attributes of industrialism discussed previously which tend to prevent individuals from leading spontaneous, self-actualizing, and purposeful lives can be seen as infringements of freedom. Some of these same attributes have a bearing upon freedom in the narrower sense of civil liberties and the relation between citizens and their government. The pace of change does not decrease as industrial societies mature, although its effects may be less apparent because the society has become more complex and differentiated. Both rapid social change and social structural complexity create problems in achieving coordination or integration of activities and produce pressures toward greater concentration of authority in both public and private organizations. The increasing number of responsibilities of government at all levels, but especially at the Federal level, is a response to this process. The New England town meeting is no longer an appropriate decision-making model in industrial societies; and although big government and big organizations do not automatically mean an infringement of individual freedom, the likelihood of an optimum balance of freedom and control from the standpoint of the individual decreases under these conditions.

The social structure of industrial society not only increases the pressure toward more centralized controls but also decreases the counterpressure for retaining individual freedom. To the extent that rapid change, structural differentiation, and lack of structural integration produce apathy and conformity, they reduce the extent of concern with freedom. Apathy decreases alertness to the infringement of civil liberties, and conformity reduces the likelihood that action will be taken even when an infringement is perceived. The fear of "getting involved" is a common symptom of apathy and conformity in industrial society.

The combination of an apathetic citizenry and an increasing necessity for extensive rationalized controls is fertile ground for the development of autocracy. In the United States and other Western democracies there are, of course, many safeguards of individual freedom built into the structure of representative government. To suggest that there is a threat to individual freedom in these societies does not imply the imminent collapse of these safeguards. We are accustomed to thinking of the loss of freedom only in terms of the overthrow of democratic regimes by totalitarian minority parties. The fact that this can happen in a mature industrial society is evidenced by the history of the Nazi party in Germany. It is often mistakenly assumed that the Nazis maintained their control of the German people exclusively through force and violence. A more accurate account appears to be that the mass of Germans were either enthusiastically "escaping from freedom," were apathetic, or were willing to conform because "you can't beat city hall." The McCarthy era in the United States is evidence that we are not immune to totalitarian pressures. And continued racial discrimination attests to the fact that our ideals regarding individual freedom are still far from being realized.

It is not, however, major confrontations of democratic and autocratic values of the sort occasioned by Senator McCarthy's accusations or the gross deficiencies in the implementation of democratic ideals, evidenced by discrimination, with which we are concerned in this section. Problems of this sort occur in both industrial and nonindustrial societies. But there is a gradual attrition of freedom, as a result of its competition with other values, which appears to be inherent in the structure of industrial society and which is therefore more centrally related to the concerns of this book. Many legitimate goals conflict with the objective of maximizing individual freedom of action. The most important one is the overriding concern in industrial society with economic growth. Efficient pursuit of this goal has, until now at least, meant increasing specialization of labor, more bureaucratic administrative procedures, and an ever-greater concentration of authority at the top of organizations that have increased in size and importance while declining in number. Although we have no way of precisely determining the optimum balance of freedom and control, it appears that even in democratic industrial societies the balance has tipped in the direction of excessive control. In the following paragraph, Erich Fromm eloquently summarizes the view of this problem presented in his book, *Escape from Freedom*:

It has been the thesis of this book that freedom has a twofold meaning for modern man: that he has been freed from traditional authorities and has become an "individual," but that at the same time he has become isolated, powerless, and an instrument of purposes outside of himself, alienated from himself and others; furthermore, that this state undermines his self, weakens and frightens him, and makes him ready for submission to new kinds of bondage. Positive freedom on the other hand is identical with the full realization of the individual's potentialities, together with his ability to live actively and spontaneously. Freedom has reached a critical point where, driven by the logic of its own dynamism, it threatens to change into its opposite. The future of democracy depends on the realization of the individualism that has been the ideological aim of modern thought since the Renaissance. The cultural and political crisis of our day is not due to the fact that there is too much individualism but that what we believe to be individualism has become an empty shell. The victory of freedom is possible only if democracy develops into a society in which the individual, his growth and happiness, is the aim and purpose of culture, in which life does not need any justification in success or anything else, and in which the individual is not subordinated to or manipulated by any power outside of himself, be it the State or the economic machine; finally, a society in which his conscience and ideals are not the internalization of external demands, but are really *his* and express the aims that result from the peculiarity of his self. These aims could not be fully realized in any previous period of modern history; they had to remain largely ideological aims, because the material basis for the development of genuine individualism was lacking. Capitalism has created this premise. The problem of production is solved—in principle at least—and we can visualize a future of abundance, in which the fight for economic privileges is no longer necessitated by economic scarcity. The problem we are confronted with today is that of the organization of social and economic forces, so that man—as a member of organized society—may become master of these forces and cease to be their slave.[27]

Although this statement was written over twenty-five years ago, the concerns it expresses are still relevant today and become even more critical as we approach the transition to postindustrial society. Unresolved social problems, conflict, and disorder are major threats to individual freedom; and these conditions are most common during periods of fundamental change in the nature of the social order. Apathy and overconformity decrease the likelihood of the reassessment of societal goals that is called for by such a period of change. In the next section we shall consider the possible effects of automation upon the structure of postindustrial society and discuss some issues affecting the probability that "the individual, his growth and happiness," will be the "aim and purpose" of postindustrial culture.

### Automation and Postindustrial Society[28]

Predicting the future of industrial society would require taking into account many current patterns of change. The extent of the population explosion, the rate of urbanization, the continuation or cessation of international tensions, and many other factors will shape the future. To predict the characteristics of postindustrial society in any detail would be an ambitious undertaking far beyond the scope of this book. However, there is an internal logic or patterning in the development of industrial technology and industrial social organization upon which some predictions about the future may be based. In Chapter 2 the development of automation was described as part of a sequence of changes in various components of production. Automation is a logical and, from the standpoint of technology, a necessary outgrowth of the technological changes that precede it. It also was described as introducing a new stage in man-machine relationships. Any basic change in the relation of men to machines is likely to affect the division of labor. The close relationship between technology and division of labor was described in both Chapters 1 and 2.

Throughout this book we have emphasized the impact of variation in the degree of division of labor upon the nature of society. The effects of the current high level of division of labor are so pervasive that they include most of the major characteristics of industrial societies. If the long-run consequence of automation is a basic change in this form of division of labor, its effects should be equally profound.

What the consequences of widespread use of automation will be still remains to be seen, and there is only a limited amount of research upon which predictions might be based. It seems likely, however, that its effect may be a reversal of the long-term trend toward increased job specialization. Automation may decrease division of labor in at least four ways. First, in a production process from which direct human involvement has been eliminated, machine monitoring and machine maintenance are almost the sole remaining functions for production workers. The task of watching or monitoring a panel of lights and gauges is basically the same, irrespective of the part of the production process involved or even the type of end product being produced. Automation thus reduces the variety of tasks to be performed.

Second, automation requires a recombination of the remaining tasks. The type of worker who is best equipped to repair and maintain automated machinery, for example, is one who has a combination of mechanical, hydraulic, electrical, and other skills. The personnel manager in one automated plant described the kind of person needed to repair automated equipment as "an engineer who is willing to get his hands dirty." It is important to note that automation does not result in job enlargement or increased skill requirements for all workers in automated industries. In spite of earlier enthusiastic predictions, it has not produced a general upgrading of industrial workers.[29] However, the integration of previously separate processing operations does have the effect of recombining tasks and is particularly likely to reduce specialization among skilled maintenance workers.

A third way in which automation may reduce division of labor is in its effect upon the structure of production organizations. There is a common managerial philosophy underlying the various applications of automation. It involves a conception of the entire production process as an integrated system and not simply as a series of steps. It has been suggested that even major divisions such as that between plant and office in manufacturing firms may be eliminated as a result of the view that they are linked together in a single interconnected system.[30] Increases in the integration of organizational structure are almost certain to produce integration of previously separate jobs into new positions involving broader responsibilities.

Finally, and perhaps most importantly, automation may decrease division of labor through its long-run effects upon distribution of employment opportunity. Earlier studies suggest that mechanization of different production components has different effects upon the structure of demand for labor.[31] Automation appears to contribute to a general shift in the labor force from more-specialized to less-specialized occupations. Some degree of specialization is characteristic of almost all work in industrial societies. In expanding professional and technical fields, however, polyvalent or generalized training is required: The practitioner is likely to identify primarily with the total occupation and only secondarily with his specialty, and the public image of the professional and technician usually involves general rather than special labels. These characteristics tend to minimize the distinction between subspecialties in these fields and have an important bearing upon the social and psychological consequences of division of labor.

We have arrived only at the early stages in the development of automation, and there have been relatively few studies of the kinds of automatic materials-handling and control systems currently in use. Although generalization based on these studies is hazardous, the available data do support the hypothesis that one consequence of automation is decreased division of labor. Robert Blauner, after an extensive analysis of interindustry differences in the nature of blue-collar jobs, concludes that "continuous process technology . . . reverses the historic trend toward greater division of labor and specialization."[32] Various case studies have shown that the elimination and recombination of tasks in automated plants result in a decrease in the number of separate job classifications. In a large automated bakery, the number of separate positions was reduced from sixteen to seven.[33] In a steel mill producing seamless pipe, automation reduced the number of job levels from seventeen to eight.[34] The following description of recombination of jobs in a highly automated power plant is a particularly dramatic example of the effect of automation upon division of labor: "The distinctions among operators in the older (non-automated) plant according to the type of equipment they operated were eliminated in the new plant. Only one class of operators was established for the new plant: power plant operators."[35]

The combination or elimination of supervisory levels is another type of decreased job specialization which often accompanies automation. This finding is reported in both the study of the seamless-pipe mill and the study of the power plant cited above. Research in a variety of other industries suggests that automation produces job enlargement in the sense of responsibility for a greater span of production.[36] Although this change does not necessarily increase either the skill level or the variety of tasks performed, it does tend to reduce the number of job classifications.

In a summary of studies dealing with the effects of automation in manufacturing plants, Floyd Mann has included the following statement, which succinctly describes the process we are concerned with here: "The integration of what were formerly discrete units of equipment also means the integration of jobs. Old boundaries between tasks are being wiped out as jobs are combined and enlarged."[37]

If automation reduces the degree of job specialization, it should also decrease alienation from work. There is some evidence that this is the case. The two major studies conducted so far that have compared workers in nonautomated plants with those in automated continuous-process plants are Robert Blauner's study of the chemical, automobile, textile, and printing industries and Floyd Mann and L. Richard Hoffman's study of electric power plants.[38] A greater commitment to work on the part of workers in more automated settings was found in both of these studies. Although there is apparently contradictory evidence from some earlier research,[39] it is important to note that these earlier studies were of factories and offices in which a high level of integration of operations through the use of centralized automatic controls had not yet occurred. In settings where this level of integration has been achieved, increased responsibility on the job, greater control over the work process, a more meaningful in-plant status structure, and more frequent teamwork apparently help to reduce the alienation of the industrial worker.

With a less-alienated work force there would be less need for bureaucratic organizational controls and greater opportunity for individual autonomy. In automated chemical and oil-refining operations, for example, workers are grouped into teams at centralized production control stations. Blauner reports that these work teams are "an effective source of work discipline" and that "men perform up to standard because they do not want to let down their workmates or their department."[40] This "inner-direction" of work behavior makes an elaborate system of external controls through rules, regulations, and supervision unnecessary in the same way that the internalized norms of workmanship in professional and skilled occupations do.

Changes in the job of the industrial worker that give him more responsibility and produce a greater commitment to work are not the only way in which automation may decrease the need for bureaucracy. Bureaucratic authority is inappropriate in organizations composed principally of professional, technical, or skilled workers; and automation is contributing to the rapid rate at which these occupations are increasing as a proportion of the labor force. The widespread use of more sophisticated computer systems will also eventually produce less bureaucratic organizational structures. Bureaucracy is a system not only for dispersing commands down through an organization but also for channeling information back up the organizational hierarchy. The greater integration of information processing made possible by computers could eliminate the need for the complex communication channels characteristic of bureaucracies.

Rationalization of industrial technology and social organization has, since the beginning of the Industrial Revolution, produced greater occupational specialization and more bureaucratized forms of organizational control. Organizational forms that may be rational in the sense of their appropriateness to organizational objectives at certain stages of technological and social structural development become irrational at other levels of development. If automation produces a reversal of the long-term trends toward social structural differentiation and bureaucratization, the result will be a society sufficiently different that it could legitimately be described as a postindustrial social order.

Among the possible effects of automation that have been described, the one likely to have the most revolutionary consequence in the long run is the shift toward a labor force composed primarily of professional, technical, and skilled workers. Although unskilled or semi-skilled manual and clerical jobs may never entirely disappear, the technological capability to eliminate most such jobs already exists and the eventual use of this capability seems inevitable. Also, the demand for teachers, engineers, scientists, doctors, nurses, medical and dental technicians, engineering technicians, skilled machine-maintenance workers, computer programmers, and many other similar occupations will continue to grow at an accelerating rate in the foreseeable future. Other occupations not now considered professions—business management, for example—are rapidly becoming professionalized in the sense that they increasingly require extensive formal training. Although it may be many years before these patterns of change in occupational distribution have run their course, it is no longer difficult to imagine a society in which most of the employees of large organizations will be professionals, technicians, or skilled tradesmen and in which most of the rest of the labor force will be engaged in some form of independent service activity.

Some hint of the extent to which such a society would differ from our own can be seen in the results of studies comparing communities with different occupational compositions. In contemporary communities having a high proportion of professionals in their labor force, there are higher rates of citizen participation in community affairs; a greater demand for medical, dental, legal, and other professional services; class, status, and power arrangements based more on education and less on manipulation of status symbols; greater use of cultural, recreational, and other leisure facilities; more concern with education as reflected both in better-financed school systems and in a higher proportion of children in school; lower birth rates; and lower rates of crime, divorce, mental illness, and other symptoms of social disorganization.[41] If a successful transition to the "age of automation" can be made, many of the social problems with which we have been concerned in this book may eventually be solved. Some of the factors that will affect the success of the transition were discussed in Chapter 2, and others will be considered in the concluding section of this chapter.

Although the major concern of this book has been with industrial society, we have also described some of the characteristics of pre-industrial society and we have now sketched some possible attributes of postindustrial society. The primary modes of production in these three types of society correspond to the three phases in man-machine relationships described in Chapter 2: craft, mechanized, and auto-mated production.[42] The social structure of any society is determined to a considerable extent by the primary way in which it produces goods and services. The transition from an agricultural, craft-based, preindustrial society to a mechanized industrial society involves a great increase in the differentiation of social structure and a decline in the level of social integration. Structural differentiation and the substitution of rational for traditional bases of social order combine to greatly accelerate the rate of social change. In the transition to an automated postindustrial society there is likely to be a decrease in social structural differentiation; and this change, along with the potentially integrative effects of computerized production control, may make possible somewhat higher levels of social integration. It is even possible that the rate of social change may decline somewhat in postindustrial society. One reason for rapid social change today is that, in societies structured around the goal of economic growth, changes in production technology have an immediate and pervasive impact. If future production systems come closer than they do now to satisfying all demands for goods and services, the major goals of postindustrial society may shift toward noneconomic concerns. Any loosening of the relationship between technology and social structure should have the effect of reducing the rate of social change.

As a consequence of differences in the primary mode of production, in the basic characteristics of social structure, and in the rate of social change, there are also differences among preindustrial, industrial, and postindustrial societies in their typical forms of social organization, in the locus of social controls, and in the relation of individuals to organizations. The dominant social organization in preindustrial society is the family, and almost all work in these societies is performed within the family or some other small owner-producer unit. Some reasons for the shift from the proprietorial form of organization to the bureaucratic form characteristic of industrial societies were presented earlier in this chapter. With the changes that will occur in the occupational distribution of the labor force in postindustrial society, the typical form of organization may be much more like those organizations today that are composed primarily of professional or skilled workers. Changes in organizational forms are closely related to change in the locus of social controls. In preindustrial small-group societies, social controls are located within the stable traditions of a fixed social order. Although the individual learns the traditional ways, and in that sense the controls upon behavior are internalized, the alternatives are so few that the individual does not emerge as the agent of choice and control is most meaningfully seen as vested in the groups within which the traditions are maintained. Industrialization frees the individual from traditional constraints, but industrial society does not provide him with opportunities for self-actualization or the development of self-image to a point where it could serve as an effective internal guide to behavior. Rational-legal and bureaucratic controls develop as substitutes for tradition and, if not welcomed, are easily tolerated by individuals with little experience in the exercise of internal controls. Changes in basic social structure, in the nature of work, and in the forms of social organization in postindustrial society may provide a more favorable social environment for the development of autonomous, inner-directed individuals. If this is so, the relation of the individual to the social

**TABLE 10. The "Main Drift"**

| Type of society | Mode of production | Basic social structural characteristics | Rate of social change | Typical form of organization | Locus of social controls | Relation of individual to organization |
|---|---|---|---|---|---|---|
| Preindustrial | Craft | Low structural differentiation<br>High social integration | Low | Proprietorial | External, traditional | No individuation |
| Industrial | Mechanized | High structural differentiation<br>Low social integration | High | Bureaucratic | External, rational | Alienation |
| Postindustrial | Automated | Moderate structural differentiation<br>Moderate social integration | Moderate | Professional | Internal | Commitment |

organizations in which he is a participant is likely to involve a sense of commitment and involvement rather than either the alienation that is characteristic in industrial society or the absence of individuation characteristic in preindustrial society.

The patterns of change just described are presented in graphic form in Table 10. The term *main drift* is borrowed from C. Wright Mills, who used it to describe some major but unplanned directions of change in contemporary society. The pattern of change suggested in Table 10 does not reflect any overall plan but rather sketches the development and further evolution of industrial society resulting from the internal logic of industrialism as a way of life. The attributes ascribed to each type of society are intended only as descriptions of central or modal tendencies in each period. It is clearly not the case, for example, that *all* individuals in industrial societies are alienated, nor are *all* organizations bureaucratically ordered. Also, the predictions about postindustrial society take into account only the technological and social structural factors with which this book has been primarily concerned; they ignore such possibilities as mass unemployment in the transition to an automated economy, population growth exceeding the world's food supply, or the culmination of international tensions in global nuclear war. The major features of contemporary industrial societies, however, have been shaped by the factors included in Table 10. It may not be unreasonable to suppose that these same factors will play an important role in determining the shape of the future.

## Social Problems of Industrial Society

This book began with the question, "How can an industrial civilization persist?" The major reason for its persistence and for the fact that it is being emulated throughout the economically underdeveloped areas of the world is that industrialism, as a cultural system, has been very effective in achieving the primary objective of industrial society—economic growth. The extent to which industrial societies are structured around this goal can be seen in the importance of work-related values for the allocation of social status, in the fact that regulation of the economy is second only to national defense as a function of government, in the widespread definition of education as vocational preparation, in the preponderance of concern with organizational needs over human needs, and in various other attributes of industrial society that have been described in this book. The affluence of mature industrial societies can scarcely be imagined by people in contemporary nonindustrial societies and would have been completely unimaginable to anyone in the seventeenth century.

Many ancient and nearly universal problems of human existence such as poverty, ignorance, and disease are on the way toward being remedied in industrial societies. As these societies mature, they become more successful in solving these problems and also those which were products of the transition from a preindustrial to an industrial social order. There are some social problems that are not solved but, in fact, become worse with the maturation of industrial society because they are inherent in its value system and social structure. Decreased working hours and alienation from work have produced a drift toward an increasingly leisure-oriented society for which the values of industrialism do not adequately prepare us either individually or collectively. Rapid technological change poses continuing problems in the adjustment of labor supply to the changing structure of labor demand.

A complex and poorly integrated status structure makes it difficult for most people to achieve or maintain a favorable and satisfying image of themselves. This problem and the role conflicts generated by a highly differentiated social structure produce generally high levels of insecurity, tension, and anxiety. Inconsequential work and inadequate preparation for leisure combine to prevent self-actualization and the development of a meaningful and purposeful life trajectory. And an elaborate system of external social controls discourages autonomy and spontaneity and encourages apathy and overconformity. In short, although industrialization has greatly improved the material well-being of man—and our concern with social problems in this book should not be construed as minimizing this accomplishment—industrialism does not permit an optimum balance of freedom and control and does not provide for the satisfaction of higher-order human needs.

Automation and postindustrial social institutions may provide an environment in which these problems can be solved. However, it would be a mistake to assume that these changes will occur either automatically or in the near future. One of the major points in Chapter 2 was that very few factories and offices today are automated; furthermore, although the shift to automation may occur more rapidly than we now anticipate, it is unlikely that the characteristics we have ascribed to postindustrial society will become a reality very soon. Nevertheless, there is no reason to wait for these changes to take place. Within the limits established by current technology, it is possible to create more meaningful occupations for many workers through the use of job-enlargement and participative-management techniques. Government programs which minimize the risks involved in the introduction of these techniques may be required to encourage their use on a broader scale. The idea, discussed at length in Chapter 3, that leisure roles may substitute for the work role as a basis for satisfying higher-order needs, suggests another approach to the solution of current problems. Education for leisure that would develop skills in creative and status-producing leisure activities could go a long way toward compensating for the stultifying nature of work in industrial societies. Our most effective deterrent to apathy, conformity, and purposelessness would appear to be formal education.

Education is important not only for solving the problems of today but also for meeting the challenges of tomorrow. The professionalization of the labor force in postindustrial society will require many more years of schooling for a much larger proportion of our population. More education also produces a broader range of capabilities and increases the capacity to adjust to a rapidly changing world of work. Vocational preparation, however, should not be the major objective of education, especially in a society in which work occupies a decreasing proportion of people's time and energy. A more appropriate but much more ambitious goal for education is the development of individuals with *whatever* skills and commitments are required to maintain self-esteem and achieve self-actualization. A related objective that may become increasingly critical for preserving democratic institutions is education that is designed to produce a better-informed electorate. Development of an educational system adequate to the needs of postindustrial society will require investment of a much greater proportion of our national resources in education. Failure to do so will not only prevent a solution to the human problems of industrial societies, it will also slow the rate of economic growth and make it impossible to retain the economic benefits that have been the major achievement of these societies.

"Men attempt to peer ahead, to understand the structure of history, to alter the process of history, if possible, in accord with their preferences . . . and the choice of men, within fairly broad limits, can shape history."[43] If we are to choose our future, we must plan for it. If we do not anticipate and prepare for problems in a rapidly changing society, the response to the resulting chaos and disorder will be a further restriction of individual freedom. Plans for the future that do not have an adequate informational and theoretical base may have the same effect. The sacrifice of freedom for control in new industrial nations today is partly a result of uncertainties regarding the outcome of planned change. A sound basis for predictions about the future will require a great expansion of social scientific research. We know very little today about the probable social and economic effects of emerging patterns of technology. Not nearly enough is known about the factors affecting population growth. Resolution of international tensions will require a much better understanding of international political processes. If we are to achieve a social order that is more consistent with human needs, we shall need to know much more about such basic social psychological processes as self-esteem maintenance and self-actualization. The application of the scientific method in sociological, psychological, and anthropological research is a comparatively recent development in the history of science. A considerable acceleration of this process will be necessary if we are to shape the future in accord with our preferences.

Effective planning requires appropriate goals as well as sound social theories and adequate information. Without the development of new, clearly defined goals, social change will be a process of drift rather than design, and the drift will almost certainly be toward a more leisure-oriented society. One effect of this drift will be a failure to complete the unfinished business of industrial society. Poverty, slums, and the social problems generated by these conditions persist despite our increasing affluence. Health facilities, and especially those for mental health, are still inadequate. Education and conservation—activities that have an important bearing upon the shape of the future—are grossly underfinanced. The probable complacency of an affluent society preoccupied with leisure pursuits would be very likely to reduce both the resources and the commitment necessary to solve these problems.

A failure to reorient the goals of industrial society may also mean that we shall fail to take advantage of opportunities provided by the transition to postindustrial society. The social problems *inherent* in industrial society stem largely from its preoccupation with the poverty that has plagued mankind throughout its history. The technology and social structure of postindustrial society may create the potential for *human* growth as well as economic growth. Realization of this potential, however, will require that individual freedom, self-respect, and self-realization become the primary goals of postindustrial society.

## FOOTNOTES

### Chapter One: Characteristics of Industrial Societies

1. Paul Meadows, *The Culture of Industrial Man*, University of Nebraska Press, Lincoln, Nebr., 1950, p. 2.
2. Frances E. Merrill, "The Study of Social Problems," *American Sociological Review*, vol. 13, pp. 251–259, June, 1948.
3. Cf. Howard S. Becker (ed.), *Social Problems*, John Wiley & Sons, Inc., New York, 1966, pp. 1–23.
4. Jessie Bernard, *Social Problems at Midcentury*, The Dryden Press, Inc., New York, 1957, pp. 90–91.
5. William A. Faunce and M. Joseph Smucker, "Industrialization and Community Status Structure," *American Sociological Review*, vol. 31, p. 393, June, 1966.
6. Cf. George M. Foster, "The Dyadic Contract: A Model for the Social Structure of a Mexican Peasant Village," *American Anthropologist*, vol. 63, pp. 1173–1192, December, 1961.
7. Emile Durkheim, *The Division of Labor in Society*, The Macmillan Company, New York, 1933.
8. Clark Kerr et al., *Industrialism and Industrial Man*, Oxford University Press, Fair Lawn, N.J., 1966, p. 221.
9. Norah T. Crowley and Daniel B. Joseph, *Industrial History*, College Entrance Book Company, New York, 1942, pp. 135–137.
10. Cf. *ibid.*, pp. 114–115.
11. Max Weber, *General Economic History*, Greenberg: Publisher Inc., New York, 1927, pp. 311–312.
12. Arthur M. Schlesinger, *Political and Social History of the United States, 1829–1925*, The Macmillan Company, New York, 1925, p. 280.
13. Quoted in Sidney Webb and Beatrice Webb, *The History of Trade Unionism*, Longmans, Green & Co., Ltd., London, 1902, p. 78.
14. Quoted in Crowley and Joseph, *op. cit.*, p. 143.
15. Karl Polanyi, *The Great Transformation*, Holt, Rinehart and Winston, Inc., New York, 1944, pp. 98–99.
16. Max Weber, *The Protestant Ethic and the Spirit of Capitalism*, George Allen & Unwin, Ltd., London, 1930.
17. *New York State Mechanic*, September 10, 1842.
18. *New York Daily Tribune*, March 22, 1854.

19. Kerr et al., *op. cit.*, pp. 221–239.
20. Cf. Webb and Webb, *op. cit.*, or John R. Commons et al., *History of Labour in the United States*, The Macmillan Company, New York, 1918.
21. Durkheim, *op. cit.*, pp. 353–373.
22. Georges Friedmann, *The Anatomy of Work*, The Free Press of Glencoe, New York, 1961, pp. 68–81.
23. For discussion of Weber's concept of rationalism, see Reinhard Bendix, "Max Weber's Interpretation of Conduct and History," *American Journal of Sociology*, vol. 51, pp. 518–526, May, 1946; H. H. Gerth and C. Wright Mills (eds.), *From Max Weber: Essays in Sociology*, Oxford University Press, Fair Lawn, N.J., 1958, pp. 51–52, 220, 293–294, 298–299; and the following works by Max Weber: *General Economic History*, pp. 312–314, 338–351; *The Theory of Social and Economic Organization*, The Fress Press of Glencoe, New York, 1947, pp. 275–278; *The Rational and Social Foundations of Music*, Southern Illinois University Press, Carbondale, Ill., 1958.
24. Included in Gerth and Mills, *op. cit.*, p. 293.

### Chapter Two: Automation and Industrial Society

1. Portions of this chapter have been adapted from the following works by William A. Faunce: "Automation and the Division of Labor," *Social Problems*, vol. 13, pp. 149–160, Fall, 1965; "Automation and Leisure," in H. B. Jacobson and J. S. Roucek (eds.), *Automation and Society*, Philosophical Library, New York, 1959, pp. 297–309; "Automation's Many Implications," *Industrial Union Department Digest*, pp. 90–99, Spring, 1959; "Professionalization and Stratification Patterns in an Industrial Community," *American Journal of Sociology*, vol. 72, pp. 341–350, January, 1967.
2. *Calling All Jobs*, National Association of Manufacturers, New York, November, 1954, p. 21.
3. Walter Reuther in *Automation and Technological Change: Hearings before the Subcommittee on Economic Stabilization of the Joint Committee on the Economic Report, Oct. 14–28, 84th Cong., First Sess.,* 1955, p. 102.
4. William A. Faunce, "Automation in the Automobile Industry: Some Consequences for In-plant and Union-management Relationships," doctoral dissertation, Wayne State University, Detroit, Mich., 1957, pp. 177–181.

5. Buckingham has described the technological developments leading to automation in a somewhat similar fashion. See Walter Buckingham, *Automation: Its Impact on Business and People*, Harper & Row, Publishers, Incorporated, New York, 1961, pp. 5–15. Both Robert Blauner and Alain Touraine have distinguished similar phases in man-machine relationships. See Robert Blauner, *Alienation and Freedom*, The University of Chicago Press, Chicago, 1964, and Alain Touraine, *L'Évolution du travail ouvrier aux usines Renault*, Centre National de la Recherche Scientifique, Paris, 1955.

6. Lewis Mumford, *Technics and Civilization*, Harcourt, Brace & World, Inc., New York, 1934, p. 10.

7. Testimony of Howard Coughlin in *Automation and Technological Change: Hearings before the Subcommittee on Economic Stabilization of the Joint Committee on the Economic Report*, Oct. 14–28, 84th Cong., First Sess., 1955, pp. 215–216. (Italics added.)

8. John I. Snyder, Jr., "The American Factory and Automation," *Saturday Review*, Jan. 22, 1955, p. 52.

9. The decline in the rate of occupational redistribution in recent years holds even when the effects of cyclical fluctuations in business activity, as measured by annual change in level of unemployment, and the effects of annual change in productivity are controlled.

10. Anderson Ashburn, "Detroit Automation," *The Annals*, vol. 340, p. 27, March, 1962.

11. Yale Brozen, "Automation's Impact on Capital and Labor Markets," in Jacobson and Roucek, *op. cit.*, p. 285.

12. National Commission on Technology, Automation, and Economic Progress, *Technology and the American Economy*, vol. I, Washington, D.C., 1966, p. 1.

13. *Ibid.*

14. *Ibid.*, vol. II, pp. 33 and 111.

15. *Ibid.*, p. 111.

16. *Ibid.*, p. 33.

17. John Diebold, "The Application of Information Technology," *The Annals*, vol. 340, p. 40, March, 1962.

18. U.S. Department of Labor, *Technological Trends in the American Economy*, 1966, p. 255.

19. Diebold, *op. cit.*, p. 45.

20. *Manpower Report of the President*, March, 1966, p. 11.

21. National Commission on Technology, Automation, and Economic Progress, *op. cit.*, vol. I, p. 16.

22. Cf. Charles C. Killingsworth, "Structural Unemployment in the United States," in Jack Stieber (ed.), *Employment Problems of Automation and Advanced Technology*, Macmillan & Co., Ltd., London, 1966, pp. 142–148.

23. *Manpower Report of the President*, p. 91.

24. *Ibid.*, p. 87.

25. A good example of the effect upon employment of the interaction between level of consumer demand and productivity growth is the declining number of farm workers. Increase in real income accompanying economic growth does not substantially increase the amount consumers spend on food; the additional money is more often used to purchase durable goods. Technologically induced growth in productivity in agriculture has occurred at a faster rate than growth in the number of people that need to be fed, and the result has been a sharp, long-term decrease in the agricultural sector of the labor force.

26. Quoted in Daniel Seligman, "The Four Day Work Week: How Soon?," *Fortune*, July, 1954, p. 83.

27. *Ibid.*, p. 114.

28. This estimate of distribution of the benefits of increased productivity is calculated as follows: Assuming that the average number of hours worked per week at some point in the past (for example, sixty-seven hours in 1870) had continued into the present, per capita income would be much higher than it is now. The difference between this figure and the present per capita income represents the amount of income "sacrificed" in order to achieve more leisure. This amount constitutes approximately 40 percent of the total benefit from increased productivity or, in other words, 40 percent of the difference between per capita income at the earlier period and the hypothetical per capita income at present if number of hours worked had not declined.

29. Bakke has noted, for example, that among working-class individuals one is regarded as successful when he has attained the standard of living customary among his associates. E. Wight Bakke, *The Unemployed Worker*, Yale University Press, New Haven, Conn., 1940, p. 20.

30. See, for example, George Lundberg et al., *Leisure*, Columbia University Press, New York, 1934, p. 123.

31. William A. Faunce, "Automation in the Automobile Industry: Some Consequences for In-plant Social Structure," *American Sociological Review*, August, 1958.

32. A study by Alfred Clarke suggests that our current concern with "spectatoritis" in American leisure patterns may be unwarranted.

Alfred C. Clarke, "The Use of Leisure and Its Relation to Levels of Occupational Prestige," *American Sociological Review*, pp. 304–305, June, 1956.

33. David Riesman, "Leisure and Work in Post-industrial Society," in Eric Larrabee and Rolf Meyersohn (eds.), *Mass Leisure*, The Free Press of Glencoe, New York, 1958, p. 366.

34. Gaylord Nelson, "Our Natural Heritage—In Danger," *I.U.D. Agenda*, pp. 3–4, August, 1966.

**Chapter Three: Alienation in Industrial Society**

1. Quoted in H. Marcuse, *Reason and Revolution*, Oxford University Press, Fair Lawn, N.J., 1941, p. 275.

2. Erich Fromm, *Marx's Concept of Man*, Frederick Ungar Publishing Co., New York, 1966, p. 44.

3. Quoted in Marcuse, *op. cit.*, p. 276.

4. Karl Marx, *Capital*, The Modern Library, Inc., New York, 1932, p. 462.

5. Quoted in Fromm, *op. cit.*, p. 98.

6. *Ibid.*, p. 56.

7. Erich Fromm, *The Sane Society*, Fawcett Publications, Inc., Greenwich, Conn., 1965, pp. 114–115.

8. *Ibid.*, pp. 111, 114.

9. Melvin Seeman, "On the Meaning of Alienation," *American Sociological Review*, vol. 24, pp. 783–791, December, 1959.

10. *Ibid.*, pp. 788–789.

11. *Ibid.*, p. 790.

12. William A. Faunce and M. Joseph Smucker, "Industrialization and Community Status Structure," *American Sociological Review*, vol. 31, pp. 390–399, June, 1966.

13. The differences among the villagers in their reactions to treatment by city dwellers were suggested by Dr. Joseph Spielberg. For a more detailed analysis of social relations in this village, see Joseph Spielberg, "San Miguel Milpas Altas: An Ethnographic Analysis of Interpersonal Relations in a Peasant Ladino Community in Guatemala," unpublished doctoral dissertation, Michigan State University, East Lansing, Mich., 1965.

14. Peter Laslett, "The World We Have Lost," in Eric Josephson and Mary Josephson (eds.), *Man Alone*, Dell Publishing Co., Inc., New York, 1962, p. 93.

15. Erich Fromm, *Escape from Freedom*, Holt, Rinehart and Winston, Inc., New York, 1941, p. 99.

16. For an analysis of the relationship of this idea to the development of capitalism, see Max Weber, *The Protestant Ethic and the Spirit of Capitalism*, Charles Scribner's Sons, New York, 1930.

17. Karl Mannheim, *Man and Society in an Age of Reconstruction*, Harcourt, Brace & World, Inc., New York, 1940, p. 59.

18. David Riesman, Nathan Glazer, and Reuel Denney, *The Lonely Crowd*, Doubleday & Company, Inc., Garden City, N.Y., 1953.

19. Cf. Robert Dubin, "Industrial Research and the Discipline of Sociology," *Proceedings of the Eleventh Annual Meeting, Industrial Relations Research Association*, 1958, pp. 152–172.

20. Everett C. Hughes, "Work and the Self," in J. Rohrer and M. Sherif (eds.), *Social Psychology at the Crossroads*, Harper & Row, Publishers, Incorporated, New York, 1951, p. 313.

21. Cf. Faunce and Smucker, *op. cit.*

22. Nancy C. Morse and Robert S. Weiss, "The Function and Meaning of Work," *American Sociological Review*, vol. 20, pp. 191–198, April, 1955.

23. Eli Chinoy, *Automobile Workers and the American Dream*, Doubleday & Company, Inc., Garden City, N.Y., 1955.

24. Herbert H. Hyman, "The Value Systems of Different Classes: A Social Psychological Contribution to the Analysis of Stratification," in Reinhard Bendix and Seymour M. Lipset, *Class, Status, and Power*, The Free Press of Glencoe, New York, 1953, pp. 426–442.

25. C. Wright Mills, *White Collar*, Oxford University Press, Fair Lawn, N.J., 1953, pp. 215–238.

26. David Riesman and Warner Bloomberg, Jr., "Work and Leisure: Fusion or Polarity?" in Conrad M. Arensberg et al., *Research in Industrial Human Relations*, Harper & Row, Publishers, Incorporated, New York, 1957, pp. 69–85.

27. Fred H. Blum, *Toward a Democratic Work Process*, Harper & Row, Publishers, Incorporated, New York, 1953, pp. 74–122.

28. Robert Dubin, "Industrial Workers' Worlds: A Study of the 'Central Life Interests' of Industrial Workers," *Social Problems*, vol. 3, pp. 131–142, January, 1956.

29. Louis H. Orzack, "Work as a 'Central Life Interest' of Professionals," *Social Problems*, vol. 7, pp. 125–132, Fall, 1959.

30. Elizabeth Lyman, "Occupational Differences in the Value Attached

to Work," *American Journal of Sociology*, vol. 61, pp. 138–144, September, 1955.

31. Harold L. Wilensky, "Varieties of Work Experience," in Henry Borow (ed.), *Man in a World at Work*, Houghton Mifflin Company, Boston, 1964, pp. 125–154.

32. Chinoy, *op. cit.*

33. Wilensky, *op. cit.*, pp. 148–149.

34. Textile workers may also experience a greater integration of work- and non-work-related social roles. Because most are employed in small, isolated, one-industry towns, work is less separated from other areas of social experience. Textile workers are also less alienated from work than would be expected on a basis of the characteristics of their jobs. See Robert Blauner, *Alienation and Freedom*, The University of Chicago Press, Chicago, 1964, pp. 58–88.

35. Cf. Blauner, *op. cit.*, pp. 124–165.

36. Louis A. Ferman, Joyce L. Kornbluh, and Alan Haber (eds.), *Poverty in America*, The University of Michigan Press, Ann Arbor, Mich., 1966, pp. 1–82.

37. The statistics reported in this section are quoted from *ibid.*, pp. 83–86.

**Chapter Four: Freedom, Control, and the Future of Industrial Society**

1. Robert Presthus, *The Organizational Society*, Alfred A. Knopf, Inc., New York, 1962, p. 75.

2. *Ibid.*, pp. 91–92.

3. *Ibid.*, pp. 205–206.

4. H. H. Gerth and C. Wright Mills (eds.), *From Max Weber: Essays in Sociology*, Oxford University Press, Fair Lawn, N.J., 1958, pp. 196–198. See also Max Weber, *The Theory of Social and Economic Organization*, Oxford University Press, Fair Lawn, N.J., 1947, pp. 324–407.

5. Arthur L. Stinchcombe, "Bureaucratic and Craft Administration of Production," *Administrative Science Quarterly*, vol. 4, pp. 168–187, September, 1959; Stanley H. Udy, Jr., " 'Bureaucracy' and 'Rationality' in Weber's Organization Theory," *American Sociological Review*, vol. 24, pp. 791–795, December, 1959. See also Helen Constas, "Max Weber's Two Conceptions of Bureaucracy," *American Journal of Sociology*, vol. 52, pp. 400–409, January, 1958.

6. Cf. William Kornhauser, *Scientists in Industry: Conflict and Accommodation*, University of California Press, Berkeley, Calif., 1962;

Simon Marcson, *The Scientist in American Industry*, Harper & Row, Publishers, Incorporated, New York, 1960; Harold Wilensky, *Intellectuals in Labor Unions*, The Free Press of Glencoe, New York, 1956.

7. Peter M. Blau and W. Richard Scott, *Formal Organizations*, Chandler Publishing Company, San Francisco, Calif., 1962, p. 209.

8. Stinchcombe, *op. cit.*, pp. 168–169.

9. Robert Blauner, *Alienation and Freedom*, The University of Chicago Press, Chicago, 1964.

10. Chris Argyris, "The Individual and Organization: An Empirical Test," *Administrative Science Quarterly*, vol. 4, p. 149, September, 1959. Items d) and g) in the list of "informal activities" in this quotation represent alienation as it has been defined in this book.

11. *Ibid.*, p. 162.

12. Robert Merton, *Social Theory and Social Structure*, The Free Press of Glencoe, New York, 1957, pp. 195–206.

13. Erich Fromm, *Escape from Freedom*, Holt, Rinehart and Winston, Inc., New York, 1941, p. 270.

14. *Ibid.*, pp. 207–239. See also Eric Hoffer, *The True Believer*, Harper & Row, Publishers, Incorporated, New York, 1951.

15. Robert Dubin, "Industrial Research and the Discipline of Sociology," *Proceedings of the Eleventh Annual Meeting of the Industrial Relations Research Association*, 1958, p. 161.

16. Chris Argyris, *Personality and Organization*, Harper & Row Publishers, Incorporated, New York, pp. 50–51.

17. Arthur Kornhauser, *Mental Health of the Industrial Worker*, John Wiley & Sons, Inc., New York, 1965.

18. *Ibid.*, p. 263.

19. William A. Faunce and M. Joseph Smucker, "Industrialization and Community Status Structure," *American Sociological Review*, vol. 31, pp. 390–399, June, 1966. See also William H. Form and Gregory P. Stone, "Urbanism, Anonymity and Status Symbolism," *American Journal of Sociology*, vol. 22, pp. 504–514, March, 1957.

20. Kornhauser, *op. cit.*, pp. 270–271.

21. Cf. *ibid.*, pp. 238–259.

22. Douglas McGregor, *The Human Side of Enterprise*, McGraw-Hill Book Company, New York, 1960, pp. 47–48.

23. Georges Friedmann, *The Anatomy of Work*, The Free Press of Glencoe, New York, 1961, pp. 20–39.

**24.** McGregor, *op. cit.*, p. 246.

**25.** A distinction can be made between the overall level of control in the social system and the distribution of control within the system. The difference between democracy and autocracy is a matter of distribution of control, whereas anarchy and its opposite represent extremes in the level of control. For an application of this distinction to the governing of trade unions, see Arnold S. Tannenbaum, "Control Structure and Union Functions," *American Journal of Sociology*, vol. 61, pp. 536–545, May, 1956.

**26.** Quoted in H. Frank Way, Jr., *Liberty in the Balance*, McGraw-Hill Book Company, New York, 1964, p. 130.

**27.** Fromm, *op. cit.*, pp. 270–271.

**28.** Portions of this section have been adapted from William A. Faunce, "Automation and the Division of Labor," *Social Problems*, vol. 13 pp. 149–160, Fall, 1965.

**29.** For a general discussion of the effect of automation on skill level, see J. R. Bright, *Automation and Management*, Harvard Graduate School of Business Administration, Division of Research, Boston, 1958.

**30.** John Diebold, "Automation as a Management Problem," in Howard B. Jacobson and Joseph S. Roucek (eds.), *Automation and Society*, Philosophical Library, Inc., New York, 1959, pp. 318–320.

**31.** Harry Jerome, *Mechanization in Industry*, National Bureau of Economic Research, Inc., New York, 1934, pp. 391–403.

**32.** Blauner, *op. cit.*, p. 143.

**33.** U.S. Department of Labor, Bureau of Labor Statistics, *A Case Study of a Large Mechanized Bakery*, 1956, p. 16.

**34.** Charles R. Walker, *Toward the Automatic Factory*, Yale University Press, New Haven, Conn., 1957, p. 61.

**35.** Floyd C. Mann and L. Richard Hoffman, *Automation and the Worker*, Holt, Rinehart and Winston, Inc., New York, 1960, p. 72.

**36.** Bright, *op. cit.*; Blauner, *op. cit.*; William A. Faunce, "The Automobile Industry: A Case Study in Automation," in Jacobson and Roucek, *op. cit.*, pp. 44–53.

**37.** Floyd C. Mann, "Psychological and Organizational Impacts," in John T. Dunlop (ed.), *Automation and Technological Change*, Prentice-Hall, Inc., Englewood Cliffs, N.J., 1962, p. 51.

**38.** Blauner, *op. cit.*; Mann and Hoffman, *op. cit.*

**39.** Ida R. Hoos, *Automation in the Office*, Public Affairs Press, Washington, D.C., 1961; Walker, *op. cit.*; Faunce, *op. cit.*

**40.** Blauner, *op. cit.*, p. 179.

**41.** Cf. William H. Form and Delbert C. Miller, *Industry, Labor, and Community*, Harper & Row, Publishers, Incorporated, New York, 1960, pp. 18–54, Paul B. Gillen, *The Distribution of Occupations as a City Yardstick*, Columbia University Press, New York, 1951; E. L. Thorndike, *Your City*, Harcourt, Brace & World, Inc., New York, 1939; Robert Cooley Angell, "The Moral Integration of American Cities," *American Journal of Sociology*, vol. 57, pp. 1–140, July, 1951; William A. Faunce and Donald A. Clelland, "Professionalization and Stratification Patterns in an Industrial Community," *American Journal of Sociology*, vol. 72, pp. 341–350, January, 1967.

**42.** The use of the term *craft* to describe the mode of production in preindustrial society does not mean that most people in such societies were skilled craftsmen in the contemporary sense; the majority of the labor force in all preindustrial societies were, and in these societies today still are, engaged in agriculture. The relationship of the farmer to the crude farm implements used in preindustrial societies is craft-like in the sense that the required skills are possessed by the farmer and not built into the tools he uses. Harvesters, threshers, and other farm machinery characteristic in industrial societies represent the change to a mechanized mode of agricultural production.

**43.** Clark Kerr et al., *Industrialism and Industrial Man*, Harvard University Press, Cambridge, Mass., 1960, p. 288.